Eucharistic Adoration

Prayers, Devotions, and Meditations

CHARLES MICHAEL

Gifted books and Media

Copyright

All rights reserved. No part of this book may be used or reproduced in any manner whatsoever without permission except in the case of brief quotations in articles, reviews, sermons, or homilies.

Scripture quotations are taken from the Douay-Rheims 1899 American Edition (Public domain)

Unless otherwise noted, scripture quotations are from Catholic Public Domain Version. Used by permission.

Compiled by Charles Michael

Printed in the United States of America

Paperback ISBN: 978-1-947343-13-9

Published by Jayclad Publishing LLC
www.giftedbookstore.com

Table of Contents

Introduction 4
Note to the Reader 5
God, the Father 6
God's Love 13
Jesus 15
Holy Spirit 30
Trinity Prayers 35
Thanksgiving 37
Word of God 49
Repentance 52
Forgiveness 58
Faith 61
Surrender 63
Deliverance 65
Healing 67
Petitions 70
Wisdom of God 73
Protection 75
Intercession 79
Ministry and Evangelization 84
Biblical Prayers 86
God's Promises 96
God's Warning about Sin and Evil 110
Why do we Adore Jesus in the Blessed Sacrament? 118
Why do we Praise God? 120

Introduction

The purpose of this book is to help us focus on God while we pray in an adoration chapel or during family prayer time. You can use it either for community prayer or for your own personal prayer. Although there is no particular order in which to recite the prayers in this book, it is recommended that you meditate regularly on each of the topics.

Christians who spend time with God daily tend to grow spiritually and have greater power over sin and evil. The problem lies in how best to spend time with God and make it effective and fruitful. People are distracted when they are left on their own to pray. In addition, they are unsure of what to pray for. This book attempts to solve this problem by giving the believer small but meaningful and relevant prayers that will help establish a connection with God. These prayers will help grow in a dynamic and loving relationship with the Almighty through Jesus and with the power of the Holy Spirit.

Charles Michael

Note to the Reader

- This book is a simple prayer guide that aims to keep our focus directed on God while we are praying either in an adoration chapel or during family prayer
- This book can be used for both community prayer and personal meditation
- If this book is used for community prayer, the pronoun "I" can be replaced with "we" in the response section of each prayer which is italicized
- There is no particular order to recite the prayers listed in this book; however, meditating on all topics given in this book regularly is recommended
- This book does not contain any traditional prayers
- Readers are encouraged to add their own intentions and petitions as and when they are inspired
- God's word is alive and active. It will bear fruit in us when we sincerely read, repeat, meditate and claim Bible verses over our life and the situations we face
- Our prayers are most effective when we live a holy, humble, and righteous life
- This book includes the basic areas of prayer which will help us to gradually use our own words to pray

God, the Father

Praises to God, the Father

Abba Father, you are omnipresent, … *I praise and worship you*
Abba Father, you are omniscient, … *I praise and worship you*
Abba Father, you are omnipotent, … *I praise and worship you*
Abba Father, you are omnibenevolent, … *I praise and worship you*
Abba Father, you are almighty, … *I praise and worship you*
Abba Father, you are sovereign, … *I praise and worship you*
Abba Father, you are all-powerful, … *I praise and worship you*
Abba Father, you are all-knowing, … *I praise and worship you*
Abba Father, you are all-seeing, … *I praise and worship you*
Abba Father, you are Jehovah Rapha, … *I praise and worship you*
Abba Father, you are Jehovah Jireh, … *I praise and worship you*
Abba Father, you are Jehovah Nissi, … *I praise and worship you*
Abba Father, you are Jehovah Elohi, … *I praise and worship you*
Abba Father, you are Jehovah Adonai, … *I praise and worship you*
Abba Father, you are Jehovah Sabaoth, … *I praise and worship you*
Abba Father, you are Jehovah shalom, … *I praise and worship you*
Abba Father, you are El Elyon, … *I praise and worship you*
Abba Father, you are Holy, … *I praise and worship you*
Abba Father, you are the righteous one, … *I praise and worship you*
Abba Father, you are eternal, … *I praise and worship you*
Abba Father, you are Spirit and truth, … *I praise and worship you*
Abba Father, you are El Shaddai, … *I praise and worship you*
Abba Father, you are God Most High, … *I praise and worship you*
Abba Father, you are Lord of Hosts, … *I praise and worship you*
Abba Father, you are the Great IAM, … *I praise and worship you*
Abba Father, Lord of heaven and earth, … *I praise and worship you*
Abba Father, you are Spirit, … *I praise and worship you*
Abba Father, you are loving, … *I praise and worship you*
Abba Father, you are merciful, … *I praise and worship you*
Abba Father, you are compassionate, … *I praise and worship you*
Abba Father, you are patient, … *I praise and worship you*
Abba Father, you are kind, … *I praise and worship you*

Abba Father, you are generous, … *I praise and worship you*
Abba Father, you are faithful, … *I praise and worship you*
Abba Father, you are trustworthy, … *I praise and worship you*
Abba Father, you are the truth, … *I praise and worship you*
Abba Father, you are perfect, … *I praise and worship you*
Abba Father, you are slow to anger, … *I praise and worship you*
Abba Father, you are gracious, … *I praise and worship you*
Abba Father, you are the revealer of mysteries , … *I praise and worship you*
Abba Father, you are the fountain of wisdom , … *I praise and worship you*
Abba Father, you are a living God, … *I praise and worship you*
God of Abraham, Isaac, and Jacob, … *I praise and worship you*
Glory be ...

Magnificat (Mother Mary's Praise to God)

My soul magnifies the Lord.

And my Spirit leaps for joy in God my Savior.

For he has looked with favor on the humility of his handmaid.

For behold, from this time, all generations shall call me blessed.

For he who is great has done great things for me, and holy is his name.

And his mercy is from generation to generations for those who fear him.

He has accomplished powerful deeds with his arm. He has scattered the arrogant in the intentions of their heart.

He has brought down the powerful from their seat, and he has exalted the humble.

He has filled the hungry with good things, and the rich he has sent away empty.

He has taken up his servant Israel, mindful of his mercy,

just as he spoke to our fathers: to Abraham and to his offspring forever.

Psalm 148 (A Psalm of Praise)

Praise the Lord from the heavens.

Praise him on the heights.

Praise him, all his Angels.

Praise him, all his hosts.

Praise him, sun and moon.

Praise him, all stars and light.

Praise him, heavens of the heavens.

And let all the waters that are above the heavens.

Praise the name of the Lord.

For he spoke, and they became.

He commanded, and they were created.

He has stationed them in eternity, and for age after age.

He has established a precept, and it will not pass away.

Praise the Lord from the earth: you sea monsters and all deep places, fire, hail, snow, ice, windstorms, which do his word.

Mountains and all hills, fruitful trees and all cedars, wild beasts and all cattle, serpents and feathered flying things.

Kings of the earth and all peoples, leaders and all judges of the earth, young men and virgins. Let the older men with the younger men, praise the name of the Lord. For his name alone is exalted.

His glory is beyond heaven and earth, and he has exalted the horn of his people. A hymn to all his holy ones, to the sons of Israel, to a people close to him. Alleluia.

Praise of Azariah and his friends (Daniel 3:52-90)

Blessed are you, Lord, God of our fathers: *praiseworthy, and glorious, and exalted above all forever.*

And blessed is the holy name of your glory: *praiseworthy, and exalted above all, for all ages.*

Blessed are you in the holy temple of your glory: *praiseworthy above all and exalted above all forever.*

Blessed are you on the throne of your kingdom: *praiseworthy above all and exalted above all forever.*

Blessed are you who beholds the abyss and sits upon the cherubim: *praiseworthy and exalted above all forever.*

Blessed are you in the firmament of heaven: *praiseworthy and glorious forever.*

All works of the Lord, bless the Lord: *praise and exalt him above all forever.*

Angels of the Lord, bless the Lord: *praise and exalt him above all forever.*

Heaven, bless the Lord: *praise and exalt him above all forever.*

All waters that are above the heavens, bless the Lord: *praise and exalt him above all forever.*

All powers of the Lord, bless the Lord: *praise and exalt him above all forever.*

Sun and moon, bless the Lord: *praise and exalt him above all forever.*

Stars of heaven, bless the Lord: *praise and exalt him above all forever.*

Every rain and dew, bless the Lord: *praise and exalt him above all forever.*

Every breath of God, bless the Lord: *praise and exalt him above all forever.*

Fire and steam, bless the Lord: *praise and exalt him above all forever.*

Cold and heat, bless the Lord: *praise and exalt him above all forever.*

Dews and frost, bless the Lord: *praise and exalt him above all forever.*

Sleet and winter, bless the Lord: *praise and exalt him above all forever.*

Ice and snow, bless the Lord: *praise and exalt him above all forever.*

Nights and days, bless the Lord: *praise and exalt him above all forever.*

Light and darkness, bless the Lord: *praise and exalt him above all forever.*

Lightning and clouds, bless the Lord: *praise and exalt him above all forever.*

May the land bless the Lord: *and praise and exalt him above all forever.*

Mountains and hills, bless the Lord: *praise and exalt him above all forever.*

All things that grow in the land, bless the Lord: *praise and exalt him above all forever.*

Fountains, bless the Lord: *praise and exalt him above all forever.*

Seas and rivers, bless the Lord: *praise and exalt him above all forever.*

Whales and all things that move in the waters, bless the Lord: *praise and exalt him above all forever.*

All things that fly in the heavens, bless the Lord: *praise and exalt him above all forever.*

All beasts and cattle, bless the Lord: *praise and exalt him above all forever.*

Sons of men, bless the Lord: *praise and exalt him above all forever.*

May Israel bless the Lord: *and praise and exalt him above all forever.*

Priests of the Lord, bless the Lord: *praise and exalt him above all forever.*

Servants of the Lord, bless the Lord: *praise and exalt him above all forever.*

Spirits and souls of the just, bless the Lord: *praise and exalt him above all forever.*

Those who are holy and humble in heart, bless the Lord: *praise and exalt him above all forever.*

Bless the Lord: *praise and exalt him above all forever.*

For he has delivered us from the underworld, and saved us from the hand of death, and freed us from the midst of the burning flame, and rescued us from the midst of the fire.

Give thanks to the Lord because he is good: *because his mercy is forever.*

All those who are pious, bless the Lord, the God of gods: *praise him and acknowledge him because his mercy is for all generations.* (Dan 3:52-90)

Scripture Meditations

The Lord is my strength and my praise, and he has become my salvation. He is my God, and I shall glorify him. He is the God of my father, and I shall exalt him. The Lord is a warrior. Almighty is his name. (Exo 15:2-3)

I will call upon the Lord, who is worthy to be praised; and I will be saved from my enemies. (2 Sam 22:4)

The Lord lives, and blessed be my rock. And the strong God of my salvation shall be exalted. (2 Sam 22:47)

Praise the Lord! Praise the Lord in his holy place. Praise him in the firmament of his power. Praise him for his mighty deeds. Praise him according to the multitude of his greatness. Praise him with the sound of the trumpet. Praise him with psaltery and stringed instrument. Praise him with timbrel and choir. Praise him with strings and organ. Praise him with sweet-sounding cymbals. Praise him with cymbals of jubilation. Let everything that breathes praise the Lord. Alleluia. (Ps 150:1-6)

O Lord, you are my God! I will exalt you, and I will praise your name. For you have accomplished wonderful things. Your plans from of old, is faithful. Amen. (Is 25:1)

Sing to the Lord a new song, sing his praise from the ends of the earth, you who descend into the sea and all its fullness, the coastlands and their inhabitants. (Is 42:10)

Blessed are you, O Lord, the God of our fathers, and your name is praiseworthy and glorious for all ages. For you are just in all the things that you have accomplished for us, and all your works are true, and your ways are right, and all your judgments are true. (Dan 3:26)

Blessing, and glory, and wisdom, and thanksgiving, and honor, and power, and might, be unto our God for ever and ever. Amen. (Rev 7:12)

O Lord, you are my God! I will exalt you, and I will praise your name. For you have accomplished wonderful things. Your plan, from of old, is faithful. (Is 25:1)

Bless the Lord, O my soul, and do not forget all his recompenses. He forgives all your iniquities. He heals all your infirmities. He redeems your life from destruction. He crowns you with steadfast love and compassion. He satisfies your desire with good things. Your youth will be renewed like that of the eagle. (Ps 103:1-5)

I will give thanks to you, Lord, with my whole heart. I will recount all your wonders. I will rejoice and exult in you. I will sing praises to your name, O Most High. (Ps 9:1-2)

Because your steadfast life is better than life itself, my lips will praise you. So will I bless you in my life, and I will lift up my hands and call on your name. (Ps 63:3-4)

For you formed my inward parts: You have knit me in my mother's womb. I will praise you; for I am fearfully and wonderfully made: marvelous are your works. (Ps 139:13-14)

My mouth is filled with praise, and I sing your glory all day long. (Ps 71:8)

I will bless the Lord at all times. His praise will be ever in my mouth. In the Lord, my soul will boast. May the meek listen and rejoice. Magnify the Lord with me, and let us extol his name together. (Ps 34:1-3)

I will extol you, O God, my king. And I will bless your name, in this time and forever and ever. Every single day, I will bless you. And I will praise your name forever and ever. The Lord is great and exceedingly praiseworthy. And there is no end to his greatness. (Ps 145:1-3)

I will always have hope. And I will praise you more and more. My mouth will announce your righteous deeds, your salvation all day long. I will come praising the mighty deeds of the Lord God, I will praise your righteousness, yours alone. (Ps 71:14-16)

Blessed are you, O Lord, the God of our fathers, and your name is praiseworthy and glorious for all ages. For you are just in all the things that you have accomplished for us, and all your works are true, and your ways are right, and all your judgments are true. (Dan 3:26-28)

God's Love

Abba Father, your love is everlasting, ... *fill me with your love*
Abba Father, your love is faithful, ... *fill me with your love*
Abba Father, your love is steadfast, ... *fill me with your love*
Abba Father, your love is eternal, ... *fill me with your love*
Abba Father, your love is unending, ... *fill me with your love*
Abba Father, your love is overflowing, ... *fill me with your love*
Abba Father, your love is redeeming, ... *fill me with your love*
Abba Father, your love is sanctifying, ... *fill me with your love*
Abba Father, your love is healing, ... *fill me with your love*
Abba Father, your love is merciful, ... *fill me with your love*
Abba Father, your love is forgiving, ... *fill me with your love*
Abba Father, your love is personal, ... *fill me with your love*
Abba Father, your love is unconditional, ... *fill me with your love*
Abba Father, your love is precious, ... *fill me with your love*
Abba Father, your love is generous, ... *fill me with your love*
Abba Father, your love is patient, ... *fill me with your love*
Abba Father, your love is comforting, ... *fill me with your love*
Abba Father, your love is renewing, ... *fill me with your love*
Abba Father, your love is reviving, ... *fill me with your love*
Abba Father, your love is consoling, ... *fill me with your love*
Abba Father, your love is caring, ... *fill me with your love*
Glory be ...

Scriptures to meditate (God's love)

God so loved the world that he gave his only-begotten Son, so that all who believe in him may not perish, but may have eternal life. (Jn 3:16)

In this is love: not as if we had loved God, but that he first loved us, and so he sent his Son as the atoning sacrifice for our sins. (1 Jn 4:10)

Though I live now in the flesh, I live in the faith of the Son of God, who loved me and who delivered himself for me. (Gal 2:20)

God proves his love for us in that, while we were yet sinners, at the proper time, Christ died for us. (Rom 5:8)

I am certain that neither death, nor life, nor Angels, nor Principalities, nor Powers, nor the present things, nor the future things, nor strength, nor the heights, nor the depths, nor any other created thing, will be able to separate us from the love of God, which is in Christ Jesus our Lord. (Rom 8:38-39)

For the mountains may depart and the hills be removed, but my steadfast love shall not depart from you. (Is 54:10)

The steadfast love of the Lord never ceases, his mercies never come to an end; they are new every morning; great is your faithfulness. (Lam 3:22-23)

Thus says the Lord who created you, O Jacob, and who formed you, O Israel: Do not be afraid. For I have redeemed you, and I have called you by your name. You are mine. (Is 43:1)

Behold, I have engraved you on my hands. Your walls are always before my eyes. (Is 49:16)

The Lord, your God, is in your midst, a warrior who gives victory; he will rejoice over you with gladness, he will renew you in his love; he will exult over you with loud singing. (Zeph 3:17)

If my father and my mother leave me behind, the Lord will take me up. (Ps 27:10)

Can a woman forget her infant, so as not to take pity on the child of her womb? But even if she would forget, still I shall never forget you. Behold, I have engraved you on my hands. Your walls are always before my eyes. (Is 49:15-16)

See how much of love the Father has given to us, that we would be called, and would become, the children of God. Because of this, the world does not know us, for it did not know God. (1 Jn 3:1)

Jesus

Praises to Jesus

Jesus, you are the bright morning star, ...*I praise and adore you*
Jesus, you are the root and descendant of David , ...*I praise and adore you*
Jesus, you are the true light, ... *I praise and adore you*
Jesus, you are the good shepherd, ... *I praise and adore you*
Jesus, you are the truth, ... *I praise and adore you*
Jesus, you are the way, ... *I praise and adore you*
Jesus, you are the life, ... *I praise and adore you*
Jesus, you are the resurrection, ... *I praise and adore you*
Jesus, you are the gate, ... *I praise and adore you*
Jesus, you are the healer, ... *I praise and adore you*
Jesus, you are the deliverer, ... *I praise and adore you*
Jesus, you are the anointed one, ... *I praise and adore you*
Jesus, you are the holy one, ... *I praise and adore you*
Jesus, you are the light of the world, ... *I praise and adore you*
Jesus, you are the most humble one, ... *I praise and adore you*
Jesus, you are meek and humble of heart, ... *I praise and adore you*
Jesus, you are the son of God, ... *I praise and adore you*
Jesus, you are the well beloved son of the father, ... *I praise and adore you*
Jesus, you are seated at the right hand of the father, ... *I praise and adore you*
Jesus, you are the Alpha and Omega, ... *I praise and adore you*
Jesus, you are the the beginning and the end, ... *I praise and adore you*
Jesus, you are the prince of peace, ... *I praise and adore you*
Jesus, you are the righteous one, ... *I praise and adore you*
Jesus, you are comforter of the afflicted, ... *I praise and adore you*
Jesus, you are the consoler of the wounded, ... *I praise and adore you*
Jesus, you are the savior of the world, ... *I praise and adore you*
Jesus, you are the redeemer of mankind, ... *I praise and adore you*
Jesus, you are the wonderful counselor, ... *I praise and adore you*
Jesus, you are the pioneer and perfecter of our faith, ... *I praise and adore you*
Jesus, you are the knowledge of God, ... *I praise and adore you*

Jesus, you are the true bread, ... *I praise and adore you*
Jesus, you are the bread from heaven, ... *I praise and adore you*
Jesus, you are the living Word, ... *I praise and adore you*
Jesus, you are the Word made flesh,... *I praise and adore you*
Jesus, you are the Word of God, ... *I praise and adore you*
Jesus, you are the second person of the trinity, ... *I praise and adore you*
Jesus, you are the wisdom of God, ... *I praise and adore you*
Jesus, you are the power of God, ... *I praise and adore you*
Jesus, you are the begotten son of the father, ... *I praise and adore you*
Jesus, you are the eternal Word, ... *I praise and adore you*
Jesus, you are the king of kings and Lord of lords, ... *I praise and adore you*
Jesus, you are the who was and who is to come, ... *I praise and adore you*
Jesus, you are the faithful witness, ... *I praise and adore you*
Jesus, you are the first born of the dead, ... *I praise and adore you*
Jesus, you are the ruler of the kings of the earth, ... *I praise and adore you*
Jesus, you are the holy one, ... *I praise and adore you*
Jesus, you are the the true one, ... *I praise and adore you*
Jesus, you are the key of David, ... *I praise and adore you*
Jesus, you are the lamb of God, ... *I praise and adore you*
Jesus, you are the author of life, ... *I praise and adore you*
Jesus, you are the Friend of sinners, ... *I praise and adore you*
Jesus, you are the lion of the tribe of Judah, ... *I praise and adore you*
Jesus, you are the atoning sacrifice, ... *I praise and adore you*
Jesus, you have the words of eternal life, ... *I praise and adore you*
Glory be ...

Jesus, you are my

Jesus, you are my God, ... *I love and adore you*
Jesus, you are my Lord, ... *I love and adore you*
Jesus, you are my love, ... *I love and adore you*
Jesus, you are my joy, ... *I love and adore you*
Jesus, you are my peace, ... *I love and adore you*
Jesus, you are my Healer, ... *I love and adore you*
Jesus, you are my deliverer, ... *I love and adore you*
Jesus, you are my consoler, ... *I love and adore you*
Jesus, you are my comforter, ... *I love and adore you*
Jesus, you are my helper, ... *I love and adore you*

Jesus, you are my friend, ... *I love and adore you*
Jesus, you are my food, ... *I love and adore you*
Jesus, you are my mediator, ... *I love and adore you*
Jesus, you are my intercessor, ... *I love and adore you*
Jesus, you are my protector, ... *I love and adore you*
Jesus, you are my provider, ... *I love and adore you*
Jesus, you are my hope, ... *I love and adore you*
Jesus, you are my savior, ... *I love and adore you*
Jesus, you are my redeemer, ... *I love and adore you*
Jesus, you are my brother, ... *I love and adore you*
Jesus, you are my master, ... *I love and adore you*
Jesus, you are my rest, ... *I love and adore you*
Jesus, you are my guardian, ... *I love and adore you*
Jesus, you are my beloved, ... *I love and adore you*
Jesus, you are my shepherd, ... *I love and adore you*
Jesus, you are my rock, ... *I love and adore you*
Jesus, you are my strength, ... *I love and adore you*
Jesus, you are my counselor, ... *I love and adore you*
Jesus, you are my refuge, ... *I love and adore you*
Jesus, you are my hiding place, ... *I love and adore you*
Jesus, you are my shield, ... *I love and adore you*
Jesus, you are my power, ... *I love and adore you*
Jesus, you are my bread, ... *I love and adore you*
Jesus, you are my wisdom, ... *I love and adore you*
Jesus, you are my security, ... *I love and adore you*
Jesus, you are my mentor, ... *I love and adore you*
Jesus, you are my desire, ... *I love and adore you*
Jesus, you are my life, ... *I love and adore you*
Jesus, you are my everything, ... *I love and adore you*
Glory be ...

Praise God with the works of Jesus

Jesus, you healed the sick, ... *I worship you*
Jesus, you gave sight to the blind, ... *I worship you*
Jesus, you forgave our sins, ... *I worship you*
Jesus, you raised the dead, ... *I worship you*
Jesus, you worked miracles, ... *I worship you*

Jesus, you cast out demons, ... *I worship you*
Jesus, you conquered the world, ... *I worship you*
Jesus, you defeated death, ... *I worship you*
Jesus, you gave us eternal life, ... *I worship you*
Jesus, you saved us from hell, ... *I worship you*
Jesus, you defeated Satan, ... *I worship you*
Jesus, you gave us freedom, ... *I worship you*
Jesus, you raised the dead, ... *I worship you*
Jesus, you gave us your body and blood, ... *I worship you*
Jesus, you founded the Church, ... *I worship you*
Jesus, you instituted the Sacraments, ... *I worship you*
Jesus, you revealed the Father to us, ... *I worship you*
Jesus, you gave us the Kingdom of God, ... *I worship you*
Jesus, you gave us the Holy Spirit, ... *I worship you*
Jesus, you continue to intercede for us, ... *I worship you*
Jesus, you judge the living and dead, ... *I worship you*
Jesus, you gave us the Word of God, ... *I worship you*
Jesus, you gave us your mother, ... *I worship you*
Jesus, you have prepared a place for us in heaven, ... *I worship you*
Glory be ...

Washing in the Blood of Jesus

Abba Father, wash me in the blood of Jesus, ... *and fill me with your Holy Spirit*
Abba Father, wash my soul in the blood of Jesus, ... *and fill me with your Holy Spirit*
Abba Father, wash my Spirit in the blood of Jesus, ... *and fill me with your Holy Spirit*
Abba Father, wash my mind in the blood of Jesus, ... *and fill me with your Holy Spirit*
Abba Father, wash my conscious mind in the blood of Jesus, ... *and fill me with your Holy Spirit*
Abba Father, wash my sub conscious in the blood of Jesus, ... *and fill me with your Holy Spirit*
Abba Father, wash my unconscious mind in the blood of Jesus, ... *and fill me with your Holy Spirit*
Abba Father, wash my heart in the blood of Jesus, ... *and fill me with your Holy Spirit*

Abba Father, wash my will in the blood of Jesus, ... *and fill me with your Holy Spirit*

Abba Father, wash my emotions in the blood of Jesus, ... *and fill me with your Holy Spirit*

Abba Father, wash my thoughts in the blood of Jesus, ... *and fill me with your Holy Spirit*

Abba Father, wash my desires in the blood of Jesus, ... *and fill me with your Holy Spirit*

Abba Father, wash my conscience in the blood of Jesus, ... *and fill me with your Holy Spirit*

Abba Father, wash my plans in the blood of Jesus, ... *and fill me with your Holy Spirit*

Abba Father, wash my ambitions in the blood of Jesus, ... *and fill me with your Holy Spirit*

Abba Father, wash my eyes in the blood of Jesus, ... *and fill me with your Holy Spirit*

Abba Father, wash my ears in the blood of Jesus, ... *and fill me with your Holy Spirit*

Abba Father, wash my speech in the blood of Jesus, ... *and fill me with your Holy Spirit*

Abba Father, wash my body in the blood of Jesus, ... *and fill me with your Holy Spirit*

Abba Father, wash my family in the blood of Jesus, ... *and fill me with your Holy Spirit*

Abba Father, wash my spouse in the blood of Jesus, ... *and fill me with your Holy Spirit*

Abba Father, wash my marriage in the blood of Jesus, ... *and fill me with your Holy Spirit*

Abba Father, wash my children in the blood of Jesus, ... *and fill me with your Holy Spirit*

Abba Father, wash my parents in the blood of Jesus, ... *and fill me with your Holy Spirit*

Abba Father, wash my home in the blood of Jesus, ... *and fill me with your Holy Spirit*

Abba Father, wash my finances in the blood of Jesus, ... *and fill me with your Holy Spirit*

Abba Father, wash my ministry in the blood of Jesus, ... *and fill me with your Holy Spirit*

Abba Father, wash my country in the blood of Jesus, ... *and fill me with your Holy Spirit*

Glory be ...

Power of the Blood of Jesus

Jesus, by your precious blood, ... *I am justified*
Jesus, by your precious blood, ... *I am atoned*
Jesus, by your precious blood, ... *I am sanctified*
Jesus, by your precious blood, ... *my sins are forgiven*
Jesus, by your precious blood, ... *I am purified*
Jesus, by your precious blood, ... *I am washed and cleansed*
Jesus, by your precious blood, ... *I am redeemed*
Jesus, by your precious blood, ... *I am protected*
Jesus, by your precious blood, ... *I am made righteous*
Jesus, by your precious blood, ... *I am set free*
Jesus, by your precious blood, ... *I have power over Satan and evil*
Glory be ...

Scriptural Rosary meditating on the Eucharist

Decade 1
Our Father...

Do not work for food that perishes, but for that which endures to eternal life, which the Son of man will give to you. (Jn 6:27)

Hail Mary...

Therefore, Jesus said to them: "Amen, amen, I say to you, Moses did not give you bread from heaven, but my Father gives you the true bread from heaven." (Jn 6:32)

Hail Mary...

The bread of God is he who descends from heaven and gives life to the world. (Jn 6:33)

Hail Mary...

They said to him, "Lord, give us this bread always." (Jn 6:34)

Hail Mary...

Jesus said to them: "I am the bread of life. Whoever comes to me shall not hunger, and whoever believes in me shall never thirst." (Jn 6:35)

Hail Mary...

I am the bread of life. (Jn 6:48)

Hail Mary...

This is the bread which descends from heaven, so that if anyone will eat from it, he may not die. (Jn 6:50)

Hail Mary...

I am the living bread, who descended from heaven. (Jn 6:51)

Hail Mary...

If anyone eats from this bread, he shall live in eternity. And the bread that I will give is my flesh, for the life of the world. (Jn 6:52)

Hail Mary...

The Jews debated among themselves, saying, "How can this man give us his flesh to eat?" (Jn 6:53)

Hail Mary...

Glory Be…

O my Jesus, forgive us our sins, save us from the fires of hell; lead all souls to heaven especially those who are in most need of Your mercy, Amen.

Decade 2
Our Father…

Jesus said to them: "Amen, amen, I say to you, unless you eat the flesh of the Son of man and drink his blood, you will not have life in you." (Jn 6:54)

Hail Mary...

Whoever eats my flesh and drinks my blood has eternal life, and I will raise him up on the last day. (Jn 6:55)

Hail Mary...

My flesh is true food, and my blood is true drink. (Jn 6:56)

Hail Mary...

Whoever eats my flesh and drinks my blood abides in me, and I in him. (Jn 6:57)

Hail Mary...

Just as the living Father has sent me and I live because of the Father, so also whoever eats me, the same shall live because of me. (Jn 6:58)

Hail Mary...

The cup of blessing that we bless, is it not a communion in the Blood of Christ? And the bread that we break, is it not a sharing in the Body of Christ? (1 Cor 10:16)

Hail Mary...

Through the one bread, we, though many, are one body: all of us who are partakers of the one bread. (1 Cor 10:17)

Hail Mary...

He rained down manna upon them to eat, and he gave them the bread of heaven. Man ate the bread of Angels. He sent them provisions in abundance. (Ps 78:24-25)

Hail Mary...

I have received from the Lord what I have also delivered to you: that the Lord Jesus, on the same night that he was handed over, took bread, and giving thanks, he broke it, and said: "Take and eat. This is my body, which shall be given up for you. Do this in remembrance of me." (1 Cor 11:23-24)

Hail Mary...

Similarly also, the cup, after he had eaten supper, saying: "This cup is the new covenant in my blood. Do this, as often as you drink it, in remembrance of me." (1 Cor 11:25)

Hail Mary...

Glory Be...

O my Jesus, forgive us our sins, save us from the fires of hell; lead all souls to heaven especially those who are in most need of Your mercy, Amen.

Decade 3
Our Father...

As often as you eat this bread and drink this cup, you proclaim the death of the Lord, until he returns. (1 Cor 11:26)

Hail Mary...

Whoever eats this bread, or drinks from the cup of the Lord, unworthily, shall be liable of the body and blood of the Lord. (1 Cor 11:27)

Hail Mary...

Examine yourself, and, only then eat from the bread, and drink from the cup. (1 Cor 11:28)

Hail Mary...

Whoever eats and drinks unworthily, eats and drinks a sentence against himself, not discerning it to be the body of the Lord. (1 Cor 11:29)

Hail Mary...

You are the temple of the living God, just as God says: "I will dwell with them, and I will walk among them. And I will be their God, and they shall be my people." (2 Cor 6:16)

Hail Mary...

While he was at table with them, he took bread, and he blessed and broke it, and he extended it to them. And their eyes were opened, and they recognized him. (Luk 24:30-31)

Hail Mary...

They continued devotedly in the apostles' teaching and fellowship, and in breaking of bread, and in prayers. (Acts 2:42)

Hail Mary...

Day by day, as they spent much time together in the temple, they broke bread at home and ate their food with glad and generous hearts, praising God and having the goodwill of all the people. And day by day the Lord added to their number those who were being saved. (Acts 2:46-47)

Hail Mary...

When the hour had arrived, he sat down at table, and the twelve Apostles with him. And he said to them: "With longing have I desired to eat this Passover with you, before I suffer." (Luk 22:14-15)

Hail Mary...

I say to you, that from this time, I will not eat it, until it is fulfilled in the Kingdom of God. (Luk 22:16)

Hail Mary...

Glory Be…

O my Jesus, forgive us our sins, save us from the fires of hell; lead all souls to heaven especially those who are in most need of Your mercy, Amen.

Decade 4
Our Father…

Having taken the chalice, he gave thanks, and he said: "Take this and share it among yourselves." (Luk 22:17)

Hail Mary...

I say to you, that I will not drink from the fruit of the vine, until the Kingdom of God arrives. (Luk 22:18)

Hail Mary...

Taking a loaf of bread, he gave thanks and broke it and gave it to them, saying: "This is my body, which is given for you. Do this in memory of me." (Luk 22:19)

Hail Mary...

Similarly also, he took the chalice, after he had eaten the meal, saying: "This chalice is the new covenant in my blood, which will be shed for you." (Luk 22:20)

Hail Mary...

They explained the things that were done on the way, and how they had recognized the Lord at the breaking of the bread. (Luk 24:35)

Hail Mary...

On the first day of the week, when we had assembled together to break bread, Paul discoursed with them, intending to set out the next day. (Acts 20:7)

Hail Mary...

He instructed the crowd to sit down on the ground. And taking the seven loaves, giving thanks, he broke and gave it to his disciples in order to distribute to the crowd and the disciples did so. (Mrk 8:6)

Hail Mary...

Melchizedek, the king of Salem, brought forth bread and wine, for he was a priest of the Most High God; he blessed him, and he said: "Blessed be Abram by the Most High God, who created heaven and earth. And blessed be the Most High God, through whose protection the enemies are in your hands." And he gave him tithes from everything. (Gen 14:18-20)

Hail Mary...

Your lamb shall be a lamb without blemish, a one year old male. You may also take it from a young goat. And you shall keep it until the fourteenth day of this month. And the entire multitude of the congregation of Israel shall slaughter it toward evening. (Exo 12:5-6)

Hail Mary...

On the next day, John saw Jesus coming toward him, and so he said: "Behold, the Lamb of God. Behold, he who takes away the sin of the world." (Jn 1:29)

Hail Mary...

Glory Be…

O my Jesus, forgive us our sins, save us from the fires of hell; lead all souls to heaven especially those who are in most need of Your mercy, Amen.

Decade 5
Our Father…

The centurion said: "Lord, I am not worthy that you should enter under my roof, but only say the word, and my servant shall be healed." (Matt 8:8)

Hail Mary…

The angel said to me: "Write: Blessed are those who have been called to the wedding feast of the Lamb." And he said to me, "These are true words of God." (Rev 19:9)

Hail Mary…

I saw, and behold, in the midst of the throne and the four living creatures, and in the midst of the elders, a Lamb was standing, as if it were slain, having seven horns and seven eyes, which are the seven spirits of God, sent forth to all the earth. (Rev 5:6)

Hail Mary…

They sang a new song: O Lord, you are worthy to take the scroll and to open its seals, because you were slain and have redeemed us for God, by your blood, from every tribe and language and people and nation. (Rev 5:9)

Hail Mary…

The crowds that preceded him, and those that followed, cried out, saying: "Hosanna to the Son of David! Blessed is he who comes in the name of the Lord. Hosanna in the highest!" (Matt 21:9)

Hail Mary…

Let us be glad and exult. And let us give glory to him. For the marriage feast of the Lamb has arrived, and his bride has prepared herself. (Rev 19:7)

Hail Mary...

While eating with them, Jesus took bread. And blessing it, he broke it and gave it to them, and he said: "Take. This is my body." (Mrk 14:22)

Hail Mary...

Having taken the chalice, giving thanks, he gave it to them. And they all drank from it. And he said to them: "This is my blood of the new covenant, which shall be shed for many." (Mrk 14:23-24)

Hail Mary...

Amen I say to you, that I will no longer drink from this fruit of the vine, until that day when I will drink it new in the Kingdom of God. (Mrk 14:25)

Hail Mary...

You nourished your people with the food of angels, and, having prepared bread from heaven, you served them without labor that which holds within itself every delight and the sweetness of every flavor. (Wis 16:20)

Hail Mary...

Glory Be…

O my Jesus, forgive us our sins, save us from the fires of hell; lead all souls to heaven especially those who are in most need of Your mercy, Amen.

Scriptures to meditate (Jesus)

I am the Way, and the Truth, and the Life. No one comes to the Father, except through me. (Jn 14:6)

The thief comes so that he may steal and kill and destroy. I have come so that they may have life, and have it more abundantly. (Jn 10:10)

Come to me, all you who labor and have been burdened, and I will give you rest. (Matt 11:28)

I am the gate. If anyone has entered through me, he will be saved. And he shall go in and go out, and he shall find pastures. (Jn 10:9)

I am the Resurrection and the Life. Whoever believes in me, even though he has died, he shall live. (Jn 11:25)

"I am the Alpha and the Omega, the Beginning and the End," says the Lord God, who is, and who was, and who is to come, the Almighty. (Rev 1:8)

I am the Alpha and the Omega, the Beginning and the End. To those who thirst, I will give freely from the fountain of the water of life. (Rev 21:6)

I am the good Shepherd. The good Shepherd gives his life for his sheep. (Jn 10:11)

I am the good Shepherd, and I know my own, and my own know me. (Jn 10:14)

He himself bore our sins in his body upon the tree, so that we, having died to sin, would live for justice. By his wounds, you have been healed. (1 Pet 2:24)

He emptied himself, taking the form of a servant, being made in the likeness of men, and accepting the state of a man. He humbled himself, becoming obedient even unto death, even the death of the Cross. (Phil 2:7-8)

He will be great, and he will be called the Son of the Most High, and the Lord God will give him the throne of David his father. (Luk 1:32)

For unto us a child is born, and unto us a son is given. And leadership is placed upon his shoulder. And his name shall be called: wonderful Counselor, mighty God, Everlasting Father, Prince of Peace. (Is 9:6)

Let us gaze upon Jesus, as the Author and the completion of our faith, who, having joy laid out before him, endured the cross, disregarding the shame, and who now sits at the right hand of the throne of God. (Heb 12:2)

I am the bread of life. Whoever comes to me shall not hunger, and whoever believes in me shall never thirst. (Jn 6:35)

He is the Lord of lords and the King of kings. (Rev 17:14)

He is the image of the invisible God, the first-born of every creature. (Col 1:15)

We do not have a high priest who is unable to have compassion on our infirmities, but rather one who was tempted in all things, just as we are, yet without sin. (Heb 4:15)

There is one God, and one mediator of God and of men, the man Christ Jesus, who gave himself as a redemption for all, as a testimony in its proper time. (1 Tim 2:5-6

Holy Spirit

Praises to the Spirit of God

Holy Spirit, ... *I praise and adore you*
Spirit of Abba Father, ... *I praise and adore you*
Spirit of Yahweh, ... *I praise and adore you*
Spirit of Christ, ... *I praise and adore you*
Spirit of God, ... *I praise and adore you*
Spirit of the Lord, ... *I praise and adore you*
Holy Spirit, the Lord, ... *I praise and adore you*
Holy Spirit, power of the Most High, ... *I praise and adore you*
Spirit of the living God, ... *I praise and adore you*
Spirit of divinity, ... *I praise and adore you*
Breadth of the Almighty, ... *I praise and adore you*
Eternal Spirit, ... *I praise and adore you*
Spirit of the Son, ... *I praise and adore you*
Spirit of love, ... *I praise and adore you*
Spirit of joy, ... *I praise and adore you*
Spirit of peace, ... *I praise and adore you*
Spirit of kindness, ... *I praise and adore you*
Spirit of faithfulness, ... *I praise and adore you*
Spirit of gentleness, ... *I praise and adore you*
Spirit of self-control, ... *I praise and adore you*
Spirit of patience, ... *I praise and adore you*
Spirit of generosity, ... *I praise and adore you*
Spirit of modesty, ... *I praise and adore you*
Spirit of chastity, ... *I praise and adore you*
Spirit of goodness, ... *I praise and adore you*
Spirit of knowledge, ... *I praise and adore you*
Spirit of wisdom, ... *I praise and adore you*
Spirit of understanding, ... *I praise and adore you*
Spirit of fortitude, ... *I praise and adore you*
Spirit of counsel, ... *I praise and adore you*
Spirit of piety, ... *I praise and adore you*
Spirit of fear of God, ... *I praise and adore you*

Spirit of word of wisdom, ... *I praise and adore you*
Spirit of word of knowledge, ... *I praise and adore you*
Spirit of prophecy, ... *I praise and adore you*
Spirit of healing, ... *I praise and adore you*
Spirit of miracles, ... *I praise and adore you*
Spirit of discernment, ... *I praise and adore you*
Spirit of faith, ... *I praise and adore you*
Spirit of tongues, ... *I praise and adore you*
Spirit of interpretation of tongues, ... *I praise and adore you*
Spirit of truth, ... *I praise and adore you*
Spirit of righteousness, ... *I praise and adore you*
Spirit of glory, ... *I praise and adore you*
Spirit of grace, ... *I praise and adore you*
Spirit of holiness, ... *I praise and adore you*
Spirit of revelation, ... *I praise and adore you*
Spirit of life, ... *I praise and adore you*
Spirit of Justice, ... *I praise and adore you*
Water of life, ... *I praise and adore you*
Holy Spirit, the helper, ... *I praise and adore you*
Holy Spirit, the advocate, ... *I praise and adore you*
Holy Spirit, the guide, ... *I praise and adore you*
Holy Spirit, the Comforter, ... *I praise and adore you*
Holy Spirit, the counselor, ... *I praise and adore you*
Holy Spirit, the Paraclete, ... *I praise and adore you*
Free Spirit, ... *I praise and adore you*
Good Spirit, ... *I praise and adore you*
Spirit of Adoption, ... *I praise and adore you*
Spirit of Judgment, ... *I praise and adore you*
Spirit of burning, ... *I praise and adore you*
Spirit of Promise, ... *I praise and adore you*
Living Waters, ... *I praise and adore you*
Glory be ...

Prayer for the Gifts and Fruits of the Holy Spirit

Come Holy Spirit, ... *fill me with the fruit of love*
Come Holy Spirit, ... *fill me with the fruit of peace*

Come Holy Spirit, ... *fill me with the fruit of joy*
Come Holy Spirit, ... *fill me with the fruit of faithfulness*
Come Holy Spirit, ... *fill me with the fruit of gentleness*
Come Holy Spirit, ...*fill me with the fruit of kindness*
Come Holy Spirit, ... *fill me with the fruit of patience*
Come Holy Spirit, ... *fill me with the fruit of generosity*
Come Holy Spirit, ... *fill me with the fruit of self-control*
Come Holy Spirit, ... *fill me with the fruit of modesty*
Come Holy Spirit, ... *fill me with the fruit of chastity*
Come Holy Spirit, ... *fill me with the fruit of goodness*
Come Holy Spirit, ... *fill me with the gift of wisdom*
Come Holy Spirit, ... *fill me with the gift of knowledge*
Come Holy Spirit, ... *fill me with the gift of understanding*
Come Holy Spirit, ... *fill me with the gift of fortitude*
Come Holy Spirit, ... *fill me with the gift of counsel*
Come Holy Spirit, ... *fill me with the gift of fear of God*
Come Holy Spirit, ... *fill me with the gift of piety*
Come Holy Spirit, ... *fill me with the charism of word of knowledge*
Come Holy Spirit, ... *fill me with the charism of word of wisdom*
Come Holy Spirit, ... *fill me with the charism of prophecy*
Come Holy Spirit, ... *fill me with the charism of healing*
Come Holy Spirit, ... *fill me with the charism of discernment*
Come Holy Spirit, ... *fill me with the charism of miracles*
Come Holy Spirit, ... *fill me with the charism of faith*
Come Holy Spirit, ... *fill me with the charism of tongues*
Come Holy Spirit, ... *fill me with the charism of interpretation of tongues*
Glory be ...

Scriptures to meditate (Holy Spirit)

I will place my Spirit within you. And I will make you walk in my precepts and keep my ordinances. (Eze 36:27)

You are not in the flesh, but in the spirit, if it is true that the Spirit of God lives within you. But if anyone does not have the Spirit of Christ, he does not belong to him. (Rom 8:9)

In the last days, says the Lord, I will pour out my Spirit, upon all flesh. And your sons and your daughters shall prophesy. And your youths shall see visions, and your elders shall dream dreams. (Acts 2:17)

This Spirit, he has poured out upon us in abundance, through Jesus Christ our Savior, so that, having been justified by his grace, we may become heirs according to the hope of eternal life. (Tit 3:6-7)

I will ask the Father, and he will give another Advocate to you, so that he may abide with you for eternity. (Jn 14:16)

Therefore, if you, being evil, know how to give good things to your sons, how much more will your Father give, from heaven, the Holy Spirit to those who ask him? (Luk 11:13)

Now the Spirit is Lord. And wherever the Spirit of the Lord is, there is liberty. (2 Cor 3:17)

The Spirit of Truth, whom the world cannot receive, because it neither perceives him nor knows him. But you shall know him. For he will remain with you, and he will be in you. (Jn 14:17)

The Spirit also helps our weakness. For we do not know how to pray as we ought, but the Spirit himself asks on our behalf with sighs too deep for words. And he who examines hearts knows what the Spirit seeks, because he asks on behalf of the saints in accordance with God. (Rom 8:26-27)

No one speaking in the Spirit of God utters a curse against Jesus. And no one is able to say that Jesus is Lord, except in the Holy Spirit. (1 Cor 12:3)

The Advocate, the Holy Spirit, whom the Father will send in my name, will teach you all things and will remind you everything whatsoever that I have said to you. (Jn 14:26)

You shall receive power when the Holy Spirit, has come over you, and you shall be witnesses for me in Jerusalem, and in all Judea and Samaria, and even to the ends of the earth. (Acts 1:8)

Whoever shall drink from the water that I will give to him will not thirst for eternity. Instead, the water that I will give to him will become in him a fountain of water, springing up into eternal life. (Jn 4:14)

When the Spirit of truth comes, he will teach the whole truth to you. For he will not be speaking from himself. Instead, whatever he will hear, he will speak. And he will announce to you the things that are to come. (Jn 16:13)

Jesus was standing and crying out, saying: "If anyone thirsts, let him come to me and drink: whoever believes in me, just as Scripture says, 'From his heart shall flow rivers of living water.' " Now he said this about the Spirit, which those who believe in him would soon be receiving. (Jn 7:37-39)

If the Spirit of him who raised up Jesus from the dead lives within you, then he who raised up Jesus Christ from the dead shall also enliven your mortal bodies, by means of his Spirit living within you. (Rom 8:11)

When the fullness of time arrived, God sent his Son, formed from a woman, formed under the law, so that he might redeem those who were under the law, in order that we might receive adoption as children. Therefore, because you are children, God has sent the Spirit of his Son into your hearts, crying out: "Abba, Father." (Gal 4:4-6)

Trinity Prayers

Consecration to the Trinity through Love

Abba Father, I love you, … *be my love* (10 times)
Abba Father, I love you, … *you are my everything* (10 times)
Abba Father, I love you, … *I belong to you* (10 times)
Abba Father, I love you, … *fill me with your love* (10 times)
Abba Father, I love you, … *you are my heart's desire* (10 times)
Abba Father, I love you, … *I surrender my life to you* (10 times)

Glory be…

Jesus, I love you, … *be my love* (10 times)
Jesus, I love you, … *you are my everything* (10 times)
Jesus, I love you, … *I belong to you* (10 times)
Jesus, I love you, … *fill me with your love* (10 times)
Jesus, I love you, … *you are my heart's desire* (10 times)
Jesus, I love you, … *I surrender my life to you* (10 times)

Glory be…

Holy Spirit, I love you, … *be my love* (10 times)
Holy Spirit, I love you, … *you are my everything* (10 times)
Holy Spirit, I love you, … *I belong to you* (10 times)
Holy Spirit, I love you, … *fill me with your love* (10 times)
Holy Spirit, I love you, … *you are my heart's desire* (10 times)
Holy Spirit, I love you, … *I surrender my life to you* (10 times)

Glory be…

Scriptures to meditate (Trinity)

Go forth and make disciples of all nations, baptizing them in the name of the Father and of the Son and of the Holy Spirit, teaching them to observe all that I have ever commanded you. And behold, I am with you always, even to the end of the age. (Matt 28:19)

Jesus, having been baptized, ascended from the water immediately, and behold, the heavens were opened to him. And he saw the Spirit of God descending like a dove, and alighting on him. And behold, there was a voice from heaven, saying: "This is my beloved Son, in whom I am well pleased." (Matt 3:16-17)

I will ask the Father, and he will give another Advocate to you, so that he may abide with you forever: the Spirit of Truth, whom the world is not able to receive, because it neither sees him nor knows him. But you shall know him. For he will remain with you, and he will be in you. (Jn 14:16-17)

The One who confirms us with you in Christ, and who has anointed us, is God. And he has sealed us, and he has placed the pledge of the Spirit in our hearts. (2 Cor 1:21-22)

The grace of our Lord Jesus Christ, and the love of God, and the communion of the Holy Spirit be with you all. Amen. (2 Cor 13:14)

In accord with the foreknowledge of God the Father, in the sanctification of the Spirit, with the obedience and the sprinkling of the blood of Jesus Christ: May grace and peace be multiplied for you. (1 Pet 1:2)

The Advocate, the Holy Spirit, whom the Father will send in my name, will teach you all things and will remind you everything whatsoever that I have said to you. (Jn 14:26)

Thanksgiving

Rosary of Thanksgiving for spiritual blessings

Decade 1
Our Father...

Thank you, Jesus, for dying on the Cross to save me
Hail Mary...

Thank you, Jesus, for taking on our sinful flesh
Hail Mary...

Thank you, Jesus, for defeating death by the cross
Hail Mary...

Thank you, Jesus, for healing our inner wounds
Hail Mary...

Thank you, Jesus, for healing our sicknesses
Hail Mary...

Thank you, Jesus, for forgiving our sins
Hail Mary...

Thank you, Jesus, for protecting us from the evil one
Hail Mary...

Thank you, Jesus, for the fruits of the Holy Spirit
Hail Mary...

Thank you, Jesus, for the gifts of the Holy Spirit
Hail Mary...

Thank you, Jesus, for the Charisms of the Holy Spirit
Hail Mary...

Glory Be...

O my Jesus, forgive us our sins, save us from the fires of hell; lead all souls to heaven especially those who are in most need of Your mercy, Amen.

Decade 2
Our Father…

Thank you, Jesus, for delivering us from evil
Hail Mary…

Thank you, Jesus, for granting us eternal life
Hail Mary…

Thank you, Jesus, for Giving us your Word
Hail Mary…

Thank you, Jesus, for Giving us the Blessed Mother
Hail Mary…

Thank you, Jesus, for giving us the Holy Spirit
Hail Mary…

Thank you, Jesus, for revealing the Father to us
Hail Mary…

Thank you, Jesus, for interceding for us
Hail Mary…

Thank you, Jesus, for teaching us
Hail Mary…

Thank you, Jesus, for freeing us from addictions
Hail Mary…

Thank you, Jesus, for giving us rest
Hail Mary…

Glory be…

O my Jesus, forgive us our sins, save us from the fires of hell; lead all souls to heaven especially those who are in most need of Your mercy, Amen.

Decade 3
Our Father…

Thank you, Jesus, for healing us, body, mind, soul, and spirit
Hail Mary…

Thank you, Jesus, for the Sacraments
Hail Mary…

Thank you, Jesus, for the Sacrament of Baptism
Hail Mary…

Thank you, Jesus, for the Sacrament of Reconciliation
Hail Mary…

Thank you, Jesus, for the Sacrament of the Eucharist
Hail Mary…

Thank you, Jesus, for the Sacrament of Confirmation
Hail Mary…

Thank you, Jesus, for the Sacrament of Holy Matrimony
Hail Mary…

Thank you, Jesus, for the Sacrament of Holy Orders
Hail Mary…

Thank you, Jesus, for the Sacrament of the anointing of the sick
Hail Mary…

Thank you, Jesus, for saving us from the fires of hell
Hail Mary…

Glory Be…

O my Jesus, forgive us our sins, save us from the fires of hell; lead all souls to heaven especially those who are in most need of Your mercy, Amen.

Decade 4
Our Father…

Thank you, Jesus, for your second coming

Hail Mary…

Thank you, Jesus, for the gift of the Eucharist
Hail Mary…

Thank you, Jesus, for gift of our Catholic faith
Hail Mary…

Thank you, Jesus, for all the priests who have ministered to me
Hail Mary…

Thank you, Jesus, for all the people who spoke to us about you
Hail Mary…

Thank you, Jesus, for your divine revelation
Hail Mary…

Thank you, Jesus, for revealing your will to us
Hail Mary…

Thank you, Jesus, for walking with us especially in times of our sufferings
Hail Mary…

Thank you, Jesus, for helping us carry our daily cross
Hail Mary…

Thank you, Jesus, for giving us the wisdom, knowledge, and the understanding to read your Word
Hail Mary…

Glory Be…

O my Jesus, forgive us our sins, save us from the fires of hell; lead all souls to heaven especially those who are in most need of Your mercy, Amen.

Decade 5
Our Father…

Thank you, Jesus, for the gift of prayer
Hail Mary…

Thank you, Jesus, for the desire for holiness
Hail Mary…

Thank you, Jesus, for the protection of our patron saint
Hail Mary…

Thank you, Jesus, for all the graces and favors
Hail Mary…

Thank you Jesus, for your protection
Hail Mary…

Thank you, Jesus, for your guidance and counsel
Hail Mary…

Thank you, Jesus, for strength during temptations
Hail Mary…

Thank you, Jesus, for the angels who protect us
Hail Mary…

Thank you, Jesus, for our guardian angel
Hail Mary…

Thank you, Jesus, for the intercession of saints
Hail Mary…

Glory Be…

O my Jesus, forgive us our sins, save us from the fires of hell; lead all souls to heaven especially those who are in most need of Your mercy, Amen.

Thanksgiving Rosary for Personal and Family Blessings

Decade 1
Our Father…

Thank you, Jesus, for the gift of Life
Hail Mary…

Thank you, Jesus, for adding another day to my life
Hail Mary…

Thank you, Jesus, for the gift of my freewill
Hail Mary…

Thank you, Jesus, for the gift of my childhood memories
Hail Mary…

Thank you, Jesus, for the gift of my family
Hail Mary…

Thank you, Jesus, for the Job and steady income in the family
Hail Mary…

Thank you, Jesus, for the gift of children
Hail Mary…

Thank you, Jesus, for my parents
Hail Mary…

Thank you, Jesus, for my siblings
Hail Mary…

Thank you, Jesus, for my grandparents
Hail Mary…

Glory Be…

O my Jesus, forgive us our sins, save us from the fires of hell; lead all souls to heaven especially those who are in most need of Your mercy, Amen.

Decade 2
Our Father…

Thank you, Jesus, for my relatives and extended family
Hail Mary…

Thank you, Jesus, for my friends and well wishers
Hail Mary…

Thank you, Jesus, for our good neighbors
Hail Mary…

Thank you, Jesus, for my daily bread
Hail Mary…

Thank you, Jesus, for my good health
Hail Mary…

Thank you, Jesus, for my home
Hail Mary…

Thank you, Jesus, for my vehicle (car)
Hail Mary…

Thank you, Jesus, for my educational qualifications
Hail Mary…

Thank you, Jesus, for my natural gifts and talents
Hail Mary…

Thank you, Jesus, for my sound mind and intellect
Hail Mary…

Glory Be…

O my Jesus, forgive us our sins, save us from the fires of hell; lead all souls to heaven especially those who are in most need of Your mercy, Amen.

Decade 3
Our Father…

Thank you, Jesus, for the good sleep each night
Hail Mary…

Thank you, Jesus, for the joy and peace we enjoy at home
Hail Mary…

Thank you, Jesus, for the financial blessings
Hail Mary…

Thank you, Jesus, for the comforts and luxuries
Hail Mary…

Thank you, Jesus, for protecting me each day
Hail Mary…

Thank you, Jesus, for all the help I have received from people
Hail Mary…

Thank you, Jesus, for purifying me through my sufferings
Hail Mary...

Thank you, Jesus, for the people who are praying for me
Hail Mary...

Thank you, Jesus, for the strength to do our daily chores
Hail Mary...

Thank you, Jesus, for protection from all sicknesses
Hail Mary...

Glory Be...

O my Jesus, forgive us our sins, save us from the fires of hell; lead all souls to heaven especially those who are in most need of Your mercy, Amen.

Decade 4
Our Father...

Thank you, Jesus, for the strength to fulfil my vocation
Hail Mary...

Thank you, Jesus, for gift of marriage (or single life)
Hail Mary...

Thank you, Jesus, for healing me
Hail Mary...

Thank you, Jesus, for all the people I met today
Hail Mary...

Thank you, Jesus, for a quiet and peaceful day
Hail Mary...

Thank you, Jesus, for making all things happen for my good
Hail Mary...

Thank you, Jesus, for preserving me from mortal sin
Hail Mary...

Thank you, Jesus, for protecting me from all dangers
Hail Mary...

Thank you, Jesus, for the ministry you have chosen for me
Hail Mary…

Thank you, Jesus, for the freedom to practice my faith
Hail Mary…

Glory Be…

O my Jesus, forgive us our sins, save us from the fires of hell; lead all souls to heaven especially those who are in most need of Your mercy, Amen.

Decade 5
Our Father…

Thank you, Jesus, for the plans you have for my welfare
Hail Mary…

Thank you, Jesus, for the help and support I receive from people
Hail Mary…

Thank you, Jesus, for the people who disciplined me for my good
Hail Mary…

Thank you, Jesus, for the sacrifices that people have made for me
Hail Mary…

Thank you, Jesus, for all the love that I receive from people
Hail Mary…

Thank you, Jesus, for your protection around all my material possessions
Hail Mary…

Thank you, Jesus, for protecting me from accidents and injuries
Hail Mary…

Thank you, Jesus, for protecting me from the evil plots of people
Hail Mary…

Thank you, Jesus, for protecting me in times of natural calamities
Hail Mary…

Thank you, Jesus, for protecting me from food, water, and airborne sickness

Hail Mary…

Glory Be…

O my Jesus, forgive us our sins, save us from the fires of hell; lead all souls to heaven especially those who are in most need of Your mercy, Amen.

Thanksgiving prayer for the religious

Thank you Jesus, for all the priests and religious
Thank you Jesus, for the priest who baptized me
Thank you Jesus, for the priest who heard my first confession
Thank you Jesus, for the priest who gave me the sacrament of my first Holy Communion
Thank you Jesus, for the priest/ bishop who gave me the Sacrament of Confirmation
Thank you Jesus, for all the priests who heard my confessions
Thank you Jesus, for the priests who celebrated masses for me
Thank you Jesus, for all the priests who have prayed for me and are praying for me
Thank you Jesus, for all the priests who have counseled me

Scriptures to meditate

Since we are receiving an immoveable kingdom, let us give thanks, by which we offer to God an acceptable worship with fear and reverence. (Heb 12:28-29)

Let the word of Christ live in you in abundance, with all wisdom, teaching and correcting one another, with psalms, hymns, and spiritual canticles, singing to God with gratitude in your hearts. (Col 3:16)

I will praise your name unceasingly, and I will praise it with thanksgiving, for my prayer was heeded. And you freed me from destruction, and you rescued me in time of trouble. (Sir 51:11)

Enter his gates with thanksgiving, his courts with praise, and acknowledge him. Bless his name. (Ps 100:4)

It might be clear to all that it is right to come before dawn to thank you, and to adore you at the dawning of the light, for the hope of the ungrateful will melt away like the winter's ice and will disperse like overflowing water. (Wis 16:28-29)

Offer to God the sacrifice of thanksgiving, and pay your vows to the Most High. (Ps 50:14)

Rejoice always. Pray without ceasing. Give thanks in everything. For this is the will of God in Christ Jesus for all of you. (1 Thes 5:18)

Rise up, my soul. Rise up, lyre and harp. I will arise in early morning. I will give thanks to you, O Lord, among the peoples. (Ps 57:8-9)

Devote yourselves to prayer. Be watchful in prayer with acts of thanksgiving. (Col 4:2)

Everything created by God is good, and nothing is to be rejected which is received with thanksgiving; for it has been sanctified by the Word of God and by prayer. (1 Tim 4:4-5)

In a day of good things, you should not be forgetful of misfortunes. And in a day of misfortunes, you should not be forgetful of good things. (Sir 11:25)

Be anxious about nothing. But in all things, with prayer and supplication, with acts of thanksgiving, let your petitions be made known to God. (Phil 4:6)

Blessed is the Lord, for he has heard the voice of my supplication. The Lord is my helper and my protector. In him, my heart has hoped and I have been helped. And my flesh has flourished again, with my song I give thanks to him. (Ps 28:6-7)

Bless the Lord, O my soul, and do not forget all his recompenses. He forgives all your iniquities. He heals all your infirmities. He redeems your life from destruction. He crowns you with mercy and compassion. He satisfies your desire with good things. (Ps 103:2-5)

I will give thanks to you, O Lord my God, with my whole heart. And I will glorify your name in eternity. For your steadfast love toward me is great, and you have rescued my soul from the lower part of Hell. (Ps 86:12-13)

Give thanks to the Lord, for he is good: for his steadfast love is eternal. (Ps 136:1)

Let them thank the Lord for his steadfast love, and for his marvelous deeds. For he has satisfied the thirsty, and he has satisfied the hungry with good things. (Ps 107:8-9)

I give you thanks, O Lord and King, and I give praise to you, O God my Savior. I acknowledge your name. For you have been my Helper and Protector. (Sir 51:1-2)

Word of God

Jesus, your word is life giving, … *fill me with your Word*
Jesus, your word is enlightening, … *fill me with your Word*
Jesus, your word heals me, … *fill me with your Word*
Jesus, your word gives me understanding, … *fill me with your Word*
Jesus, your word counsels me, … *fill me with your Word*
Jesus, your word comforts me, … *fill me with your Word*
Jesus, your word encourages me, … *fill me with your Word*
Jesus, your word disciplines me, … *fill me with your Word*
Jesus, your word is law to me, … *fill me with your Word*
Jesus, your word delivers me, … *fill me with your Word*
Jesus, your word saves me, … *fill me with your Word*
Jesus, your word redeems me, … *fill me with your Word*
Jesus, your word fills me with knowledge, … *fill me with your Word*
Jesus, your word gives me wisdom, … *fill me with your Word*
Jesus, your word restores me, … *fill me with your Word*
Jesus, your word cleanses me, … *fill me with your Word*
Jesus, your word is truth, … *fill me with your Word*
Jesus, your word increases my faith, … *fill me with your Word*
Jesus, your word casts out the devil, … *fill me with your Word*
Jesus, your word teaches me, … *fill me with your Word*
Jesus, your word anoints me, … *fill me with your Word*
Jesus, I meditate on your Word day and night, … *fill me with your Word*
Jesus, your word is a lamp to my feet, … *fill me with your Word*
Jesus, your word is a light to my path, … *fill me with your Word*
Jesus, your word is good news to me, … *fill me with your Word*
Jesus, your word is the sword of the Spirit, … *fill me with your Word*
Jesus, your word gives me joy, … *fill me with your Word*
Jesus, your word strengthens me, … *fill me with your Word*
Jesus, your word is peace, … *fill me with your Word*
Jesus, your word frees me from sin and evil, … *fill me with your Word*
Jesus, your word is revelation to me, … *fill me with your Word*
Glory be …

Biblical prayers

I am your servant. Give me understanding, so that I may know your decrees. (Ps 119:125)

I have rejoiced in the way of your commands, more than in all riches. I will meditate in your precepts, and examine your ways. I will delight myself in your statutes: I will not forget your word. (Ps 119:14-16)

Your word is a lamp to my feet and a light to my path. (Ps 119:105)

I rejoice at your word, as one that finds great spoil. I hate and abhor lying: but I love your law. (Ps 119:162-163)

I meditated on your commandments, which I loved. And I lifted up my hands to your commandments, which I loved. (Ps 119:47-48)

How have I loved your law, O Lord? It is my meditation all day long. (Ps 119:97)

I have acquired your decrees as an inheritance unto eternity, because they are the joy of my heart. I have inclined my heart to perform your statutes for eternity, as a recompense. (Ps 119:111-112)

I will rejoice over your words, like one who has found many spoils. (Ps 119:161)

Scriptures to meditate

The book of this law shall not depart from your mouth. Instead, you shall meditate upon it, day and night, so that you may observe and do all the things that are written in it. Then you shall direct your way and understand it. (Josh 1:8)

Heaven and earth shall pass away, but my words shall not pass away. (Matt 24:35)

As rain and snow descend from heaven, and do not return there until they have soaked the earth, and watered it, and causing it to bloom and to provide seed to the sower and bread to the hungry, so also will my word be, which will go forth from my mouth. It will not return to me empty, but it will accomplish whatever I will, and it will prosper in the tasks for which I sent it. (Is 55:10-11)

Blessed is the man who has not followed the counsel of the wicked, and has not remained in the way of sinners, and has not sat in the chair of scoffers. But his will is with the law of the Lord, and he will meditate on his law, day and night. (Ps 1:1-2)

The law of the Lord is perfect, reviving souls. The testimony of the Lord is faithful, providing wisdom to little ones; the justice of the Lord are right, rejoicing hearts; the precepts of the Lord is clear, enlightening the eyes. (Ps 19:7-8)

Indeed, neither an herb, nor a poultice, healed them, but your word, O Lord, which heals all. (Wis 16:12)

My child, pay attention to what I say, and incline your ear to my words. Let them not recede from your eyes. Keep them in the midst of your heart. For they are life to those who find them and health to all that is flesh. (Pro 4:20-22)

Is not my word like fire, says the Lord, and like a hammer that breaks a rock in pieces? (Jer 23:29)

If you will abide in my word, you will truly be my disciples. And you shall know the truth, and the truth shall set you free. (Jn 8:31-32)

Man shall not live by bread alone, but by every word that proceeds from the mouth of God. (Matt 4:4)

All Scripture, having been divinely inspired, is useful for teaching, for reproof, for correction, and for instruction in justice, so that the man of God may be perfect, having been trained for every good work. (2 Tim 3:16-17)

I have hidden your word in my heart, so that I may not sin against you. (Ps 119:11)

Repentance

Prayer of Repentance

For the sin of idolatry, ... *Jesus have mercy on me and forgive me*
For the sin of disobedience, ... *Jesus have mercy on me and forgive me*
For the sin of stubbornness, ... *Jesus have mercy on me and forgive me*
For the sin of rebelliousness, ... *Jesus have mercy on me and forgive me*
For the sin of blasphemy, ... *Jesus have mercy on me and forgive me*
For the sin of unbelief, ... *Jesus have mercy on me and forgive me*
For not praying every day, ... *Jesus have mercy on me and forgive me*
For not reading the Bible every day, ... *Jesus have mercy on me and forgive me*
For the sin of superstition, ... *Jesus have mercy on me and forgive me*
For the sin of occult activities, ... *Jesus have mercy on me and forgive me*
For loving anything more than you, ... *Jesus have mercy on me and forgive me*
For taking the Lord's name in vain, ... *Jesus have mercy on me and forgive me*
For not using my talents for the glory of God, ... *Jesus have mercy on me and forgive me*
For profaning the Lord's day, ... *Jesus have mercy on me and forgive me*
For missing Mass on Sundays, ... Jesus have mercy on me and forgive me
For the sin of dishonoring our parents, ... *Jesus have mercy on me and forgive me*
For not loving others unconditionally, ... *Jesus have mercy on me and forgive me*
For the sin of abortion, ... *Jesus have mercy on me and forgive me*
For the sin of murder, ... *Jesus have mercy on me and forgive me*
For the sin of racism, ... *Jesus have mercy on me and forgive me*
For the sin of discrimination and favoritism, ... *Jesus have mercy on me and forgive me*
For the sin of smoking, ... *Jesus have mercy on me and forgive me*
For the sin of alcohol addiction, ...*Jesus have mercy on me and forgive me*
For the sin of drug addiction, ...*Jesus have mercy on me and forgive me*
For the sin of Adultery, ...*Jesus have mercy on me and forgive me*
For the sin of fornication, ...*Jesus have mercy on me and forgive me*

For the sin of pornography, …*Jesus have mercy on me and forgive me*
For the sin of masturbation, …*Jesus have mercy on me and forgive me*
For all sexual sins, …*Jesus have mercy on me and forgive me*
For the sin of worldliness, …*Jesus have mercy on me and forgive me*
For wasting or misusing time, …*Jesus have mercy on me and forgive me*
For entertaining wrong desires, …*Jesus have mercy on me and forgive me*
For not tithing, …*Jesus have mercy on me and forgive me*
For being stingy and miserly, …*Jesus have mercy on me and forgive me*
For the sin of lying, …*Jesus have mercy on me and forgive me*
For the sin of boasting, …*Jesus have mercy on me and forgive me*
For the sin of gossiping, …*Jesus have mercy on me and forgive me*
For the sin of false accusation, …*Jesus have mercy on me and forgive me*
For the sin of false witnessing, …*Jesus have mercy on me and forgive me*
For not helping the poor, …*Jesus have mercy on me and forgive me*
For coveting others' property, …*Jesus have mercy on me and forgive me*
For desiring for what is not mine, …*Jesus have mercy on me and forgive me*
For the sin of pride, …*Jesus have mercy on me and forgive me*
For the sin of envy, …*Jesus have mercy on me and forgive me*
For the sin of anger, …*Jesus have mercy on me and forgive me*
For the sin of sloth, …*Jesus have mercy on me and forgive me*
For the sin of lust, …*Jesus have mercy on me and forgive me*
For the sin of gluttony, …*Jesus have mercy on me and forgive me*
For the sin of greed, …*Jesus have mercy on me and forgive me*
For all my hidden sins, …*Jesus have mercy on me and forgive me*
For sins of omission, …*Jesus have mercy on me and forgive me*
For my sinful thoughts, …*Jesus have mercy on me and forgive me*
For my sinful words, …*Jesus have mercy on me and forgive me*
For my sinful actions, …*Jesus have mercy on me and forgive me*
Glory be …

Psalm 51 (Biblical prayer of repentance)

Have mercy on me, O God, according to your steadfast love. And, according to the multitude of your compassion, blot out my transgressions.

Wash me thoroughly from my iniquity, and cleanse me from my sin.

For I know my iniquity, and my sin is ever before me.

Against you alone have I sinned, and I have done evil before your eyes. And so, you are justified in your words, and blameless when you give judgment.

For behold, I was born in guilt, and in sinfulness did my mother conceive me.

For behold, you have loved truth in the inward parts. therefore teach me wisdom in my secret heart.

You will sprinkle me with hyssop, and I will be cleansed. You will wash me, and I will be made whiter than snow.

Let me hear gladness and rejoicing. And the bones that have been crushed will exult.

Turn your face away from my sins, and erase all my iniquities.

Create a clean heart in me, O God. And renew an upright spirit within my inmost being.

Do not cast me away from your presence; and do not take your Holy Spirit from me.

Restore to me the joy of your salvation, and confirm me with a willing spirit.

Then I will teach the unjust your ways, and the impious will be converted to you.

Deliver me from bloodshed, O God, the God of my salvation, and my tongue will extol your justice.

O Lord, you will open my lips, and my mouth will announce your praise.

For if you had desired sacrifice, I would certainly have given it, but with burnt offerings, you will not be delighted.

A crushed spirit is a sacrifice to God. A contrite and broken heart, O God, you will not spurn.

Act kindly, Lord, in your good will toward Zion, so that the walls of Jerusalem may be built up.

Psalm 32:1-5

Blessed are they whose iniquities have been forgiven and whose sins have been covered.

Blessed is the man to whom the Lord has not imputed sin, and in whose spirit there is no deceit.

Because I was silent, my bones wasted away, while I cried out all day long.

For, day and night, your hand was heavy upon me; my strength withered as in dry summer heat..

Then I acknowledged my sin to you, and I did not conceal my iniquity.

I said, "I will confess my sins to the Lord," and you forgave the guilt of my sin.

Ps 103: 8-14

The Lord is compassionate and merciful, patient and full of steadfast love

He will not be angry forever, and he will not always accuse.

He has not dealt with us according to our sins, and he has not repaid us according to our iniquities.

For according to the height of the heavens above the earth, so great is his steadfast love toward those who fear him.

As far as the east is from the west, so far has he removed our iniquities from us.

As a father is compassionate to his children, so has the Lord been compassionate to those who fear him.

For he knows how we were made. He remembers that we are dust.

Biblical prayers for God's mercy

Jesus, Master, have mercy on us. (Luk 17:13)

God be merciful to me a sinner. (Luk 18:13)

Lord, be merciful to me; heal me, for I have sinned against you. (Ps 41:4)

Act of contrition

O my God, I am heartily sorry for having offended you, and I detest all my sins because of your just punishments, but most of all because they offend you, my God, who are all good and deserving of all my love. I firmly resolve with the help of your grace to sin no more and to avoid the near occasion of sin. Amen.

Scriptures to meditate

If my people, over whom my name has been invoked, humble themselves, will have petitioned me and sought my face, and will have repented for their wicked ways, then I will heed them from heaven, and I will forgive their sins, and I will heal their land. (2 Chron 7:14)

Let us examine our ways, and seek out, and return to the Lord. Let us lift up our hearts, with our hands, toward the Lord in the heavens. (Lam 3:40-41)

If the impious man does penance for all his sins which he has committed, and if he keeps all my precepts, and accomplishes judgment and justice, then he shall certainly live, and he shall not die. (Eze 18:27)

The time has been fulfilled and the kingdom of God has drawn near. Repent and believe in the Gospel. (Mrk 1:15)

As I live, says the Lord God, I do not desire the death of the impious, but that the impious should convert from his way and live. Be converted, be converted from your evil ways! For why should you die, O house of Israel? (Eze 33:11)

Draw near to God, and he will draw near to you. Cleanse your hands, you sinners! And purify your hearts, you double-minded! Be afflicted: mourn and weep. Let your laughter be turned into mourning, and your gladness into sorrow. (Jas 4:8-9)

"But even now," says the Lord, "repent sincerely and return to me with fasting and weeping and mourning. Be converted to me with your whole heart, in fasting and weeping and mourning. And rend your hearts, and not your garments, and convert to the Lord your God. (Joel 2:12-13)

Return to the Lord, and forsake your sins. Make supplication in the presence of the Lord, and diminish your offenses. Return to the Lord, and turn away from your sins, and have immense hatred for what he hates. (Sir 17:25-26)

Thus says the Lord of hosts, the God of Israel: Make your ways and your intentions good, and I will live with you in this place. (Jer 7:3)

Return, each one from his evil way, and from your wicked thoughts. And you shall dwell in the land, which the Lord has given to you and to your ancestors, from ancient times and forever. (Jer 25:4)

I will give them a heart, so that they may know me, that I am the Lord. And they will be my people, and I will be their God. For they shall return to me with their whole heart. (Jer 24:7)

Let us examine our ways, and seek out, and return to the Lord. Let us lift up our hearts, with our hands, toward the Lord in the heavens. (Lam 3:40-41)

From the days of your ancestors, you have withdrawn from my ordinances and have not kept them. Return to me, and I will return to you, says the Lord of hosts. (Mal 3:7)

If you will return to me, and keep my precepts, and do them, even if you will have been led away to the furthest reaches of the heavens, I will gather you from there, and I will lead you back to the place that I have chosen so that my name would dwell there. (Neh 1:9)

Repent and turn to God, so that your sins may be wiped away. So then, the times of refreshing will come from the presence of the Lord, and he will send the One who was foretold to you, Jesus Christ. (Acts 3:19-20)

If we confess our sins, then he is faithful and just, so as to forgive us our sins and to cleanse us from all iniquity. (1 Jn 1:9)

Do you despise the riches of his goodness and patience and forbearance? Do you not know that the kindness of God is calling you to repentance? (Rom 2:4)

Forgiveness

Forgiveness Prayer

All those who mocked me, ...*Jesus, I forgive*
All those who rejected me, ...*Jesus, I forgive*
All those who hate me, ...*Jesus, I forgive*
All those who hurt me physically, ...*Jesus, I forgive*
All those who hurt me emotionally, ... *Jesus, I forgive*
All those who condemned me, ...*Jesus, I forgive*
All those who misunderstood me, ...*Jesus, I forgive*
All those who discriminated me, ...*Jesus, I forgive*
All those who cheated me, ... *Jesus, I forgive*
All those who abused me, ... *Jesus, I forgive*
All those who ignored me, ...*Jesus, I forgive*
All those who neglected me, ...*Jesus, I forgive*
All those who slandered me, ...*Jesus, I forgive*
All those who abandoned me, ... *Jesus, I forgive*
All those who deceived me, ... *Jesus, I forgive*
All those who conspired against me, ... *Jesus, I forgive*
All those who stole from me, ... *Jesus, I forgive*
All those who gossiped against me, ...*Jesus, I forgive*
All those who falsely accused me, ...*Jesus, I forgive*
All those who treat me as enemies, ...*Jesus, I forgive*
For all the sins that my parents committed against me, ...*Jesus, I forgive*
For all the sins that my spouse committed against me, ...*Jesus, I forgive*
For all the sins that my children committed against me, ...*Jesus, I forgive*
For all the sins that my friends committed against me, ...*Jesus, I forgive*
For all sins that my coworkers committed against me, ...*Jesus, I forgive*
For all the sins that my superiors committed against me, ...*Jesus, I forgive*
For all the sins that the Church (religious people) committed against me, ...*Jesus, I forgive*...
Glory be...

Prayer for enemies

Jesus have mercy on my enemies, ... *and bless them*

Jesus have mercy on those who hate me, ... *and bless them*
Jesus have mercy on those who abuse me, ... *and bless them*
Jesus have mercy on all who persecute me, ... *and bless them*
Jesus have mercy on all who cheated me, ... *and bless them*
Jesus have mercy on all who ignore me, ... *and bless them*
Jesus have mercy on all who plot and conspire against me, ... *and bless them*
Jesus have mercy on those who mocked me, ... *and bless them*
Jesus have mercy on those who discriminate me, ... *and bless them*
Jesus have mercy on those who hurt me, ... *and bless them*
Jesus have mercy on those who rejected me, ... *and bless them*
Jesus have mercy on those slandered against me, ... *and bless them*
Jesus have mercy on those rejoiced at my downfall, ... *and bless them*
Jesus have mercy on those who maligned me, ... *and bless them*
Jesus have mercy on those who obstructed my success, ... *and bless them*
Jesus have mercy on those who betrayed me, ... *and bless them*
Jesus have mercy on those who insulted me, ... *and bless them*
Jesus have mercy on those who spread falsehood about me, ... *and bless them.* ...
Glory be…

Scriptures to meditate

If you will forgive men their sins, your heavenly Father also will forgive you your offenses. But if you will not forgive men, neither will your Father forgive you your sins. (Matt 6:14-15)

When you stand to pray, if you hold anything against anyone, forgive them, so that your Father, who is in heaven, may also forgive you your sins. But if you will not forgive, neither will your Father, who is in heaven, forgive you your sins. (Mrk 11:25-26)

If one has no mercy toward another like himself, can he then seek pardon for his own sins? (Sir 28:4)

Forgive your neighbor, if he has harmed you, and then your sins will be forgiven you when you pray. (Sir 28:2)

Do not judge, and you will not be judged. Do not condemn, and you will not be condemned. Forgive, and you will be forgiven. (Luk 6:37)

If you offer your gift at the altar, and there you remember that your brother has something against you, leave your gift there, before the altar, and go first to be reconciled to your brother, and then you may approach and offer your gift. (Matt 5:23-24)

Be reconciled with your adversary quickly, while you are still on the way with him, lest perhaps the adversary may hand you over to the judge, and the judge may hand you over to the officer, and you will be thrown in prison. Amen I say to you, that you shall not go forth from there, until you have repaid the last penny. (Matt 5:25-26)

Bless those who persecute you: bless, and do not curse. Rejoice with those who are rejoicing. Weep with those who are weeping. (Rom 12:14-15)

Love your enemies. Do good to those who hate you. And pray for those who persecute and slander you. (Matt 5:44)

If your enemy is hungry, feed him. If he is thirsty, give him water to drink. For you will gather hot coals upon his head, and the Lord will repay you. (Pro 25:21-22)

If an enemy is hungry, feed him; if he is thirsty, give him a drink. For in doing so, you will heap burning coals upon his head. Do not allow evil to prevail, instead prevail over evil by means of goodness. (Rom 12:20-21)

You shall not hate your brother in your heart, but reprove him openly, lest you have sin over him. Do not seek revenge, neither should you be mindful of the injury of your fellow citizens. You shall love your friend as yourself. I am the Lord. (Lev 19:17-18)

Then his lord called him, and he said to him: 'You wicked servant, I forgave you all your debt, because you pleaded with me. Therefore, should you not also have had compassion on your fellow servant, just as I also had compassion on you?' And his lord, being angry, handed him over to the torturers, until he repaid the entire debt. So, too, shall my heavenly Father do to you, if each one of you will not forgive his brother from your hearts. (Matt 18:32-35)

Be kind and merciful to one another, forgiving one another, just as God has forgiven you in Christ. (Eph 4:32)

Faith

Lord Jesus, increase my faith, … *where there is unbelief*
Lord Jesus, increase my faith, … *where there is doubt*
Lord Jesus, increase my faith, … *where there is confusion*
Lord Jesus, increase my faith, … *where there is despair*
Lord Jesus, increase my faith, … *where there is uncertainity*
Lord Jesus, increase my faith, … *where there is decision making*
Lord Jesus, increase my faith, … *where there is no hope*
Lord Jesus, increase my faith, … *in times of financial difficulties*
Lord Jesus, increase my faith, … *in times of failures*
Lord Jesus, increase my faith, … *in times of my weaknesses*
Lord Jesus, increase my faith, … *in times of sicknesses*
Lord Jesus, increase my faith, … *in times of suffering and hardship*
Lord Jesus, increase my faith, … *in times of persecution*
Lord Jesus, increase my faith, … *when I am rejected*
Lord Jesus, increase my faith, … *when I feel unloved*
Lord Jesus, increase my faith, … *when I feel spiritually dry*
Lord Jesus, increase my faith, … *when thing don't go my way*
Lord Jesus, increase my faith, … *when my prayers are not answered*
Lord Jesus, increase my faith, … *when I am weak and tired*
Lord Jesus, increase my faith, … *when I am impatient*
Lord Jesus, increase my faith, … *when I have sinned*
Lord Jesus, increase my faith, … *when I am sad and depressed*
Lord Jesus, increase my faith, … *when I am crushed and brokenhearted*
Lord Jesus, increase my faith, … *when I am troubled and distressed*
Lord Jesus, increase my faith, … *when I have committed a mortal sin*
Lord Jesus, increase my faith, … *when I am faced with an impossible situation*
Lord Jesus, increase my faith, … *when I am worried and anxious*
Lord Jesus, increase my faith, … *when I am fearful*
Lord Jesus, increase my faith, … *when I am unable to forgive*
Lord Jesus, increase my faith, … *when I am filled with hatred and bitterness*
Lord Jesus, increase my faith, … *when I am filled with sinful thoughts*
Lord, I believe, help my unbelief
Lord, I believe, help my unbelief
Lord, I believe, help my unbelief
Glory be…

Scriptures to meditate

All things whatsoever that you ask for when praying: believe that you have received it, and it will be yours. (Mrk 11:24)

All that is born of God overcomes the world. And this is the victory that overcomes the world: our faith. (1 Jn 5:4)

All things are possible for the one who believes. (Mrk 9:23)

Lord, I believe. Help my unbelief. (Mrk 9:24)

We walk by faith, and not by sight. (2 Cor 5:7)

Ask with faith, doubting nothing. For he who doubts is like a wave on the ocean, which is moved about by the wind and carried away, must not expect to receive anything from the Lord. (Jas 1:6-8)

Without faith, it is impossible to please God. For whoever approaches God must believe that he exists, and that he rewards those who seek him. (Heb 11:6)

Truly I say to you, if you will have faith like a grain of mustard seed, you will say to this mountain, 'Move from here to there,' and it shall move. And nothing will be impossible for you. (Matt 17:20)

Faith is the assurance of things hoped for, the evidence of things not seen. (Heb 11:1)

I can do all things through Christ who strengthens me. (Phil 4:13)

If you confess with your mouth the Lord Jesus, and if you believe in your heart that God has raised him up from the dead, you shall be saved. (Rom 10:9)

For in Christ Jesus, neither circumcision nor uncircumcision prevails over anything, but only faith which works through love. (Gal 5:6)

Surrender

Prayer of surrender

Jesus, into your hands, I give my life, … *fill me with your peace*
Jesus, into your hands, I give my worries, … *fill me with your peace*
Jesus, into your hands, I give my anxieties, … *fill me with your peace*
Jesus, into your hands, I give my fears, … *fill me with your peace*
Jesus, into your hands, I give my impatience, … *fill me with your peace*
Jesus, into your hands, I give my anger, … *fill me with your peace*
Jesus, into your hands, I give my disappointments, … *fill me with your peace*
Jesus, into your hands, I give my victories, … *fill me with your peace*
Jesus, into your hands, I give my failures, … *fill me with your peace*
Jesus, into your hands, I give my weaknesses, … *fill me with your peace*
Jesus, into your hands, I give my temptations, … *fill me with your peace*
Jesus, into your hands, I give my sin, … *fill me with your peace*
Jesus, into your hands, I give my addictions, … *fill me with your peace*
Jesus, into your hands, I give my frustrations, … *fill me with your peace*
Jesus, into your hands, I give my negative thoughts, … *fill me with your peace*
Jesus, into your hands, I give my pain, … *fill me with your peace*
Jesus, into your hands, I give my sufferings, … *fill me with your peace*
Jesus, into your hands, I give my insecurities, … *fill me with your peace*
Jesus, into your hands, I give my thoughts, … *fill me with your peace*
Jesus, into your hands, I give my desires, … *fill me with your peace*
Jesus, into your hands, I give my ambitions, … *fill me with your peace*
Jesus, into your hands, I give my future, … *fill me with your peace*
Jesus, into your hands, I give my financial needs, … *fill me with your peace*
Jesus, into your hands, I give my ambitions, … *fill me with your peace*
Jesus, into your hands, I give my brokenness, … *fill me with your peace*
Jesus, into your hands, I give my sicknesses, … *fill me with your peace*
Jesus, into your hands, I give my vocation, … *fill me with your peace*
Jesus, into your hands, I give my ministry, … *fill me with your peace*
Jesus, into your hands, I give my family, … *fill me with your peace*
Glory be…

Scriptures to meditate

He was separated from them by about a stone's throw. And kneeling down, he prayed, saying: "Father, if you are willing, take this chalice away from me. Yet truly, let not my will, but yours, be done." Then an Angel appeared to him from heaven, strengthening him. (Luk 22:41-43)

Cast all your anxiety upon him, for he takes care of you. (1 Pet 5:7)

By faith, Abraham, when he was tested, offered Isaac, so that he who had received the promises was offering up his only son. (Heb 11:17)

Mary said: "Behold, I am the handmaid of the Lord. Let it be done to me according to your word." (Luk 1:38)

A leper, drawing near, adored him, saying, "Lord, if you choose, you can make me clean." And Jesus, extending his hand, touched him, saying: "I am willing. Be cleansed." And immediately his leprosy was cleansed. (Matt 8:2-3)

I say to you, do not worry about your life, as to what you will eat, nor about your body, as to what you will wear. Is not life more than food, and the body more than clothing? (Matt 6:25-26)

Deliverance

Deliverance prayer

From all sin causing spirits, …*Jesus deliver me*
From all sickness causing spirits, …*Jesus deliver me*
From the deception of Satan, …*Jesus deliver me*
From the spirit of worldliness, …*Jesus deliver me*
From all negative spirits, …*Jesus deliver me*
From all demons and evil spirits, …*Jesus deliver me*
From all addictions, …*Jesus deliver me*
From addictions to the digital and social media, …*Jesus deliver me*
From all substance addictions, …*Jesus deliver me*
From the sin of the flesh, …*Jesus deliver me*
From all curses against me, …*Jesus deliver me*
From all sinful company and friendships, …*Jesus deliver me*
From the habit of gossiping, …*Jesus deliver me*
From all judgmental thoughts …*Jesus deliver me*
From habit of lying, …*Jesus deliver me*
From profanity in speech, …*Jesus deliver me*
From selfish and unholy desires, …*Jesus deliver me*
From the lust of the eyes, …*Jesus deliver me*
From the sin of complaining and grumbling, …*Jesus deliver me*
From all lustful thoughts, …*Jesus deliver me*
From any unforgiveness, … *Jesus deliver me*
From hatred, bitterness, and resentment, … *Jesus deliver me*
From the spirit of oppression, … *Jesus deliver me*
From the spirit of fear, … *Jesus deliver me*
From the spirit of anger, … *Jesus deliver me*
From the spirit of worry and anxiety, … *Jesus deliver me*
From the spirit of sorrow and sadness, … *Jesus deliver me*
From the spirit of doubt and confusion, … *Jesus deliver me*
From the spirit of stubbornness, … *Jesus deliver me*
Glory be…

Scriptures to Meditate (Deliverance)

Behold, I have given you authority to tread upon snakes and scorpions, and upon all the powers of the enemy, and nothing will hurt you. (Luk 10:19)

Having called together his twelve disciples, he gave them authority over unclean spirits, to cast them out and to cure every sickness and every infirmity. (Matt 10:1)

Behold, they brought him a man who was mute, having a demon. And after the demon was cast out, the mute man spoke. And the crowds wondered, saying, "Never has anything like this been seen in Israel." (Matt 9:32-33)

Jesus of Nazareth, whom God anointed with the Holy Spirit and with power, traveled around doing good and healing all those oppressed by the devil. For God was with him. (Acts 10:38)

They cried out to the Lord in their tribulation, and he freed them from their distress. And he led them out of darkness and the shadow of death, and he broke apart their chains. (Ps 107:13-14)

For if he is a true child of God, he will help him and deliver him from the hands of his adversaries. (Wis 2:18)

He has rescued us from the power of darkness, and he has transferred us into the kingdom of his beloved Son. (Col 1:13)

He delivered me, because he delighted in me. (Ps 18:19)

His burden will be taken away from your shoulder, and his yoke will be taken away from your neck. (Is 10:27)

Healing

Healing Prayer

Jesus, have mercy on me, ... *and heal me*
Jesus, have mercy on me, ... *and heal my soul*
Jesus, have mercy on me, ... *and heal my body*
Jesus, have mercy on me, ... *and heal my mind*
Jesus, have mercy on me, ... *and heal my heart*
Jesus, have mercy on me, ... *and heal my thoughts*
Jesus, have mercy on me, ... *and heal my intellect*
Jesus, have mercy on me, ... *and heal my reasoning*
Jesus, have mercy on me, ... *and heal my will*
Jesus, have mercy on me, ... *and heal my emotions*
Jesus, have mercy on me, ... *and heal my memories*
Jesus, have mercy on me, ... *and heal my conscience*
Jesus, have mercy on me, ... *and heal my senses*
Jesus, have mercy on me, ... *and heal my family*
Jesus, have mercy on me, ... *and heal all my relationships*
Jesus, have mercy on me, ... *and heal my spouse*
Jesus, have mercy on me, ... *and heal my children*
Jesus, have mercy on me, ... *and heal my parents*
Jesus, have mercy on me, ... *and heal my siblings*
Jesus, have mercy on me, ... *and heal my enemies*
Jesus, have mercy on me, ... *and heal my coworkers*
Jesus, have mercy on me, ... *and heal the whole world*
Glory be...

Biblical prayers of healing

Heal me, O Lord, and I will be healed. Save me, and I will be saved. For you are my praise. (Jer 17:14)

O Lord my God, I have cried out to you, and you have healed me. (Ps 30:2)

Have mercy on me, Lord, for I am weak. Heal me, Lord, for my bones are shaking with terror, and my soul has been very troubled. (Ps 6:2-3)

Scriptures to meditate

In your infirmity, you should not neglect yourself, but pray to the Lord, and he will heal you. (Sir 38:9)

Is anyone ill among you? Let him bring in the priests of the Church, and let them pray over him, anointing him with oil in the name of the Lord. (Jas 5:14)

I saw his ways, and I healed him, and I led him back again, and I restored consolations to him and to those who mourn for him. I created the fruit of the lips: peace, peace to him who is far away, and peace to him who is near, said the Lord, and I healed him. (Is 57:18-19)

He himself was wounded because of our iniquities. He was bruised because of our wickedness. The discipline of our peace was upon him. And by his wounds, we are healed. (Is 53:5)

When the sun had set, all those who had anyone afflicted with various diseases brought them to him. Then, laying his hands on each one of them, he cured them. (Luk 4:40)

Jesus traveled throughout all of the cities and towns, teaching in their synagogues, and preaching the Gospel of the kingdom, and healing every illness and every infirmity. (Matt 9:35)

The entire crowd was trying to touch him, because power went out from him and healed all. (Luk 6:19)

Bless the Lord, O my soul, and do not forget all his benefits. He forgives all your iniquities. He heals all your infirmities. (Ps 103:2-3)

A multitude also hurried to Jerusalem from the neighboring cities, carrying the sick and those troubled by unclean spirits, who were all healed. (Acts 5:16)

Many followed him, and he cured them all. (Matt 12:15)

O Lord my God, I cried to you for help, and you have healed me. O Lord, you brought up my soul from Sheol, restored me to life from among those gone down to the Pit. (Ps 30:1-2)

Behold, I will lead over them recovery and health, and I will cure them. And I will reveal to them an abundance of prosperity and security. (Jer 33:6)

But unto you, who fear my name, the Sun of justice will arise, and health will be in his wings. And you will go forth and leap like the calves of the herd. (Mal 4:2)

If you will listen to the voice of the Lord your God, and do what is right in his sight, and obey his commands, and keep all his precepts, I will not bring upon you any of the diseases that I brought upon Egypt. For I am the Lord, your healer. (Exo 15:26)

You shall serve the Lord your God, so that I may bless your bread and your waters, and so that I may take away sickness from your midst. There will not be fruitless or barren ones in your land. I will fill up the number of your days. (Exo 23:25-26)

When the people of that place had recognized him, they sent word into all that region, and they brought to him all who were sick. And they begged him, so that they might touch even the hem of his garment. And as many as touched it were healed. (Matt 14:35-36)

Jesus of Nazareth, whom God anointed with the Holy Spirit and with power, traveled around doing good and healing all those oppressed by the devil. For God was with him. (Acts 10:38)

Petitions

Abba Father, have mercy on me, ... *and fill me with your love*
Abba Father, have mercy on me, ... *and fill me with your joy*
Abba Father, have mercy on me, ... *and fill me with your peace*
Abba Father, have mercy on me, ... *and fill me with your presence*
Abba Father, have mercy on me, ... *and increase my faith*
Abba Father, have mercy on me, ... *and fill me with your Holy Spirit*
Abba Father, have mercy on me, ... *and fill me with wisdom*
Abba Father, have mercy on me, ... *and fill me with the fruits of the Holy Spirit*
Abba Father, have mercy on me, ... *and fill me with the gifts of the Holy Spirit*
Abba Father, have mercy on me, ... *and fill me with Charisms of the Holy Spirit*
Abba Father, have mercy on me, ... *and forgive my sins*
Abba Father, have mercy on me, ... *and heal my body, mind, and soul*
Abba Father, have mercy on me, ... *and wash me in the blood of Jesus*
Abba Father, have mercy on me, ... *and bless me*
Abba Father, have mercy on me, ... *and make me holy*
Abba Father, have mercy on me, ... *and restore me*
Glory be...

Prayer to make us more like Jesus

Jesus, make me humble, ... *and use me for your glory*
Jesus, make me holy, ... *and use me for your glory*
Jesus, make me pure, ... *and use me for your glory*
Jesus, make me wise, ... *and use me for your glory*
Jesus, make me loving, ... *and use me for your glory*
Jesus, make me joyful, ... *and use me for your glory*
Jesus, make me peaceful, ... *and use me for your glory*
Jesus, make me kind, ... *and use me for your glory*
Jesus, make me faithful, ... *and use me for your glory*
Jesus, make me gentle, ... *and use me for your glory*
Jesus, make me patient, ... *and use me for your glory*
Jesus, make me contrite, ... *and use me for your glory*
Jesus, make me repentant, ... *and use me for your glory*

Jesus, make me merciful, ... *and use me for your glory*
Jesus, make me compassionate, ... *and use me for your glory*
Jesus, make me perfect, ... *and use me for your glory*
Jesus, make me generous, ... *and use me for your glory*
Jesus, make me obedient, ... *and use me for your glory*
Jesus, make me simple, ... *and use me for your glory*
Jesus, make me prudent, ... *and use me for your glory*
Jesus, make me content, ... *and use me for your glory*
Jesus, make me meek, ... *and use me for your glory*
Jesus, make me modest, ... *and use me for your glory*
Jesus, make me good, ... *and use me for your glory*
Jesus, make me to do your will,... *and use me for your glory*
Glory be...

Scriptures to meditate

Things to ask God everyday

Pray to know God's will
This is the confidence which we have toward God: that no matter what we shall request, in accord with his will, he hears us. (1 Jn 5:14)

Pray for faith
The Apostles said to the Lord, "Increase our faith." (Luk 17:5)

Pray for the Holy Spirit
Ask, and it shall be given to you. Seek, and you shall find. Knock, and it shall be opened to you. For everyone who asks, receives; and whoever seeks, finds; and to anyone who knocks, it will be opened. (Matt 7:7-8)

Pray for wisdom
If anyone among you is in need of wisdom, let him petition God, who gives abundantly to all without reproach, and it shall be given to him. (Jas 1:5)

Pray for direction and counsel
Concerning all things, pray to the Most High, so that he may direct your way in truth. (Sir 37:15)

Pray for God's presence
One thing I asked of the Lord, that will I seek after: to live in the house of the Lord all the days of my life, to behold the beauty of the Lord, and to inquire in his temple. (Ps 27:4)

Pray to be filled with God's love
But may God our Father himself, and our Lord Jesus Christ, direct our way to you. And may the Lord multiply you, and make you abound in your love toward one another and toward all. (1 Thes 3:11-12)

Pray for God's forgiveness
For you are good and forgiving, Lord, and plentiful in steadfast love to all who call upon you. (Ps 86:5)

Pray for your needs (petitions)
Be anxious about nothing. But in all things, with prayer and supplication, with acts of thanksgiving, let your petitions be made known to God. (Phil 4:6)

Pray for God's mercy
Be merciful to me, O God, according to your steadfast love. And, according to your abundant mercy, wipe out my iniquity. Wash me once again from my iniquity, and cleanse me from my sin. (Ps 51:1-2)

Pray for healing
In your infirmity, you should not neglect yourself, but pray to the Lord, and he will cure you. (Sir 38:9)

Pray before making major decisions
Therefore, David consulted the Lord, saying, "Shall I go and strike down these Philistines?" And the Lord said to David, "Go, and you shall strike down the Philistines, and you shall save Keilah." (1 Sam 23:2)

Pray for the gifts of the Holy Spirit
Pursue love. Be zealous for spiritual things, and especially so that you may prophesy. (1 Cor 14:1)

Wisdom of God

Daily prayer for Godly and divine wisdom

Jesus, fill me with your divine wisdom, ... *to discern good and evil*
Jesus, fill me with your divine wisdom, ... *to handle my money and finances*
Jesus, fill me with your divine wisdom, ... *in saying the right words*
Jesus, fill me with your divine wisdom, ... *to understand spiritual things*
Jesus, fill me with your divine wisdom, ... *to avoid sin*
Jesus, fill me with your divine wisdom, ... *and help me with my education*
Jesus, fill me with your divine wisdom, ... *to understand and interact with people*
Jesus, fill me with your divine wisdom, ... *to lead and manage my family (for husbands)*
Jesus, fill me with your divine wisdom, ... *to manage my household (for wives)*
Jesus, fill me with your divine wisdom, ... *to understand my parents and be obedient to them (for children)*
Jesus, fill me with your divine wisdom, ... *to raise my children (for parents)*
Jesus, fill me with your divine wisdom, ... *to know my role in the family and fulfill it*
Jesus, fill me with your divine wisdom, ... *to understand God's will*
Jesus, fill me with your divine wisdom, ... *to understand and obey God's Word*
Jesus, fill me with your divine wisdom, ... *in all my actions*
Jesus, fill me with your divine wisdom, ... *to use my time wisely*
Jesus, fill me with your divine wisdom, ... *to be effective at my workplace or business*
Jesus, fill me with your divine wisdom, ... *when making decisions*
Glory be...

Scriptures to meditate

If anyone among you is in need of wisdom, let him petition God, who gives abundantly to all without reproach, and it shall be given to him. (Jas 1:5)

All wisdom is from the Lord God, and has always been with him, and is before all time. (Sir 1:1)

Possess wisdom, for it is better than gold. And acquire prudence, for it is more precious than silver. (Pro 16:16)

Wisdom is pure and never fades away, and is easily seen by those who love her and found by those who seek her. (Wis 6:12)

I chose, and understanding was given to me; and I prayed, and the spirit of wisdom came to me. (Wis 7:7)

For if you would call upon wisdom and bend your heart to prudence, if you will seek her like money, and dig for her as if for treasure, then you will understand the fear of the Lord, and you will discover the knowledge of God. (Pro 2:3-5)

I love those who love me. And those who stand watch for me until morning shall discover me. (Pro 8:17)

The fear of the Lord is the beginning of wisdom. A good understanding is for all who do it. His praise remains from age to age. (Ps 111:10)

Wisdom will not enter into a malicious soul, nor dwell in a body subdued by sin. (Wis 1:4)

My child, If you desire wisdom, observe the commandments, and then God will lavish her upon you. (Sir 1:26)

Set your thoughts on the precepts of God, and be entirely constant in his commandments. And he himself will give you insight, and the desire of wisdom will be given to you. (Sir 6:37)

My son, pay attention to my wisdom, and incline your ear to my prudence, so that you may guard your thinking, and so that your lips may preserve discipline. (Pro 5:1-2)

All good things came to me along with her, and innumerable wealth by her hand; and I rejoiced in all these, because this wisdom leads them. (Wis 7:11-12)

Protection

Prayer of protection

From the viles of the devil, ... *Jesus, protect me*
From the lies of the devil, ... *Jesus, protect me*
From the deception of the devil, ... *Jesus, protect me*
From evil and wicked people, ... *Jesus, protect me*
From sinful people, ... *Jesus, protect me*
From all dangers, ... *Jesus, protect me*
From accidents and injury, ... *Jesus, protect me*
From natural calamities, ... *Jesus, protect me*
From people who tempt me to sin, ... *Jesus, protect me*
From scandals and controversies, ... *Jesus, protect me*
From unforeseen illnesses, ... *Jesus, protect me*
During my weak moments, ... *Jesus, protect me*
From the consequences of wrong decisions, ... *Jesus, protect me*
From the consequences of my sin, ... *Jesus, protect me*
From all evil spiritual forces and demons, ... *Jesus, protect me*
From all air, water borne, and food related illnesses, ... *Jesus, protect me*
Jesus, protect my spouse,... *and keep him/her safe*
Jesus, protect my children,... *and keep them safe*
Jesus, protect my parents,... *and keep them safe*
Jesus, protect my siblings,... *and keep them safe*
Jesus, protect all my family members,... *and keep them safe*
Jesus, protect all my friends and well wishers,... *and keep them safe*
Jesus protect all my coworkers,... *and keep them safe*
Jesus all my prayer group members,... *and keep them safe*
Jesus protect all the religious,... *and keep them safe*
Glory be...

Sealing Prayer

I cover myself, ... *with the cross of Jesus*
I cover myself, ... *with the wounds of Jesus*

I cover myself, ... *with the blood of Jesus*
I cover myself, ... *with the light of Jesus*
I cover myself, ... *with the love of Jesus*
I cover myself, ... *with the mercy of Jesus*
I cover myself, ... *with the spirit of Jesus*
I cover myself, ... *with the grace of Jesus*
I cover myself, ... *with the truth of Jesus*
I cover myself, ... *with the righteousness of Jesus*
I cover myself, ... *with the shield of faith*
I cover myself, ... *with the helmet of salvation*
I cover myself, ... *with the shoes of peace*
I cover myself, ... *with the belt of truth*
I cover myself, ... *with the sword of the Spirit, the word of God*
Glory be...

Psalm 91 (God's promise of protection)

He who dwells in the secret place of the most High shall abide under the shadow of the Almighty, will say of the Lord, He is my refuge and my fortress: my God; in him will I trust.

He shall deliver you from the snare of the fowler, and from the deadly pestilence.

He shall cover you with his feathers, and under his wings you will find refuge: his faithfulness shall be a shield and buckler.

You shall not be afraid for the terror by night; nor for the arrow that flies by day; Nor for the pestilence that walks in darkness; nor for the destruction that wastes at noonday.

A thousand shall fall at your side, and ten thousand at your right hand; but it shall not come near you. Only with your eyes shall you behold and see the reward of the wicked.

Because you have made the Lord, your refuge, the most High, your dwelling place; No evil befall you, neither shall any plague come near your dwelling.

For he shall give his angels charge over you, to keep you in all your ways. They shall bear you up in their hands, lest you dash your foot against a stone.

You shall tread upon the lion and adder: the young lion and the serpent, you shall trample under feet.

Those who love me, I will deliver him: I will protect him, because he knows my name.

He shall call upon me, and I will answer him: I will be with him in trouble; I will deliver him, and honor him.

With long life will I satisfy him, and show him my salvation.

Armor of God prayer (Eph 6:10-17)

Finally, be strong in the Lord, and in the power of his might.

Put on the whole armor of God, so that you may be able to stand against the wiles of the devil.

For we wrestle not against flesh and blood, but against principalities, against powers, against the rulers of the darkness of this world, against spiritual wickedness in high places.

Therefore take unto you the whole armor of God, so that you may be able to withstand in the evil day, and having done everything, to stand firm.

Stand therefore, having your loins girded with the belt of truth, and having on the breastplate of righteousness;

And for your feet put on whatever will prepare you for the proclamation of the gospel of peace;

Above all, taking the shield of faith, with which you shall be able to quench all the fiery darts of the wicked.

And take the helmet of salvation, and the sword of the Spirit, which is the word of God. (Eph 6:10-17)

Scriptures to meditate

The Lord is your keeper, the Lord is your protection, at your right hand. The sun will not burn you by day, nor the moon by night. The Lord guards you from all evil. May the Lord guard your soul. May the Lord guard your entrance and your exit, from this time forward and even forever. (Ps 121:5-8)

God is faithful. He will strengthen you, and he will guard you from the evil one. (2 Thes 3:3)

You are my hiding place; You preserve me from trouble; You encompass me with songs of deliverance. (Ps 32:7)

But you, Lord, are my shield, my glory, and the one who raises up my head. I have cried out to the Lord with my voice, and he has heard me from his holy mountain. (Ps 3:3-4)

Intercession

General intercession prayer

Jesus, have mercy on the sick, ... *and fill them with your Holy Spirit*
Jesus, have mercy on the mentally ill, ...
Jesus, have mercy on the orphans, ...
Jesus, have mercy on the homeless, ...
Jesus, have mercy on the hungry, ...
Jesus, have mercy on the poor, ...
Jesus, have mercy on those who are oppressed by the devil, ...
Jesus, have mercy on those who are affected by natural calamities, ...
Jesus, have mercy on those who have lost a loved one, ...
Jesus, have mercy on those who are in danger, ...
Jesus, have mercy on those who are weak and are being tempted, ...
Jesus, have mercy on all those who are depressed, ...
Jesus, have mercy on all those with suicidal tendencies, ...
Jesus, have mercy on those who are suffering, ...
Jesus, have mercy on those who are in pain, ...
Jesus, have mercy on those who are bedridden, ...
Jesus, have mercy on those who are dying with terminal illness, ...
Jesus, have mercy on those who are physically challenged, ...
Jesus, have mercy on those who are hospitalized, ...
Jesus, have mercy on those who are undergoing surgery, ...
Jesus, have mercy on those who have met with an accident, ...
Jesus, have mercy on those who are tired and lethargic, ...
Jesus, have mercy on all those who are addicted to smoking, ...
Jesus, have mercy on all those who are addicted to alcohol, ...
Jesus, have mercy on all those who are addicted to drugs, ...
Jesus, have mercy on all those who watch pornography, ...
Jesus, have mercy on all those who are in the porn industry, ...
Jesus, have mercy on all those who commit the sin of masturbation, ...
Jesus, have mercy on all those fornicate, ...
Jesus, have mercy on all those who commit adultery, ...
Jesus, have mercy on all those who engage in homosexual acts, ...
Jesus, have mercy on all the rapists and molesters, ...

Jesus, have mercy on all the pedophiles, …
Jesus, have mercy on all the atheists and agnostics, …
Jesus, have mercy on all those who practice occult, …
Jesus, have mercy on all those who believe in superstition, …
Jesus, have mercy on all the people of other religions, …
Jesus, have mercy on all the murderers, …
Jesus, have mercy on all those who have committed abortion, and those who aid in abortion, …
Jesus, have mercy on all the thieves, robbers, scammers, and hackers, …
Jesus, have mercy on all the terrorists, …
Jesus, have mercy on all those who persecute Christians,
Jesus, have mercy on all those who do not pray or read the bible, …
Jesus, have mercy on all those who are worldly, …
Jesus, have mercy on all the fallen away catholics, …
Jesus, have mercy on all the Christian denominations, …
Jesus, have mercy on those who don't go for Mass, …
Jesus, have mercy on those who don't confess their sins, …
Jesus, have mercy on the Church, …
Jesus, have mercy on the Holy Father, …
Jesus, have mercy on all the cardinals and bishops, …
Jesus, have mercy on all the priests, …
Jesus, have mercy on our parish priest, …
Jesus, have mercy on all the seminarians, …
Jesus, have mercy on all the retreat centers, …
Jesus, have mercy on all lay people involved in ministry, …
Jesus, have mercy on all religious orders and religious houses, …
Jesus, have mercy on all families, …
Jesus, have mercy on all marriages, …
Jesus, have mercy on all those who are divorced, separated, on the verge of separation, …
Jesus, have mercy on all little children, …
Jesus, have mercy on all teenagers, …
Jesus, have mercy on all old people, …
Jesus, have mercy on all childless couples, …
Jesus, have mercy on all families with financial problems, …
Jesus, have mercy on all the single people who are finding it difficult to find a life partner, …
Jesus, have mercy on our president (leader), …
Jesus, have mercy on all the lawmakers and politicians of our country, …
Jesus, have mercy on all the world leaders, …

Jesus, have mercy on the media, …
Glory be…

Intercession for the sick

Jesus, heal all the sick, … *and fill them with your Holy Spirit*
Jesus, heal all the diabetics, …
Jesus, heal all those suffering from high blood pressure, …
Jesus, heal all those suffering from migraine and chronic headaches, …
Jesus, heal all those suffering from AIDS, …
Jesus, heal all those suffering from lupus, …
Jesus, heal all those suffering from Epilepsy, …
Jesus, heal all those suffering from Schizophrenia, …
Jesus, heal all those suffering from bipolar disorder, …
Jesus, heal all those suffering from OCD, …
Jesus, heal all those suffering from Arthritis, …
Jesus, heal all those suffering from fibromyalgia, …
Jesus, heal all those suffering from MS, …
Jesus, heal all those suffering from Parkinson's disease, …
Jesus, heal all those suffering from autism, …
Jesus, heal all those suffering from ADHD, …
Jesus, heal all those suffering from down syndrome, …
Jesus, heal all the children suffering from learning disabilities, …
Jesus, heal all those suffering from Leukemia, …
Jesus, heal all those suffering from cancer, …
Jesus, heal all those suffering from down syndrome, …
Jesus, heal all the blind, …
Jesus, heal all those suffering from hearing loss, …
Jesus, heal all those suffering from migraine and severe headaches, …
Jesus, heal all those suffering from sexually transmitted diseases, …
Jesus, heal all those suffering from various skin diseases, …
Jesus, heal all those who are bedridden, …
Jesus, heal all those who are physically challenged, …
Jesus, heal all those suffering from various incurable diseases, …
Jesus, heal all those suffering from unknown sicknesses, …
Glory be…

Intercession for the religious

Jesus, have mercy on all those who work for your kingdom, ... *and fill them with your Holy Spirit*
Jesus, have mercy on the Holy Father, ...
Jesus, have mercy on all the Cardinals, ...
Jesus, have mercy on all the Bishops, ...
Jesus, have mercy on all the priests, ...
Jesus, have mercy on the religious nuns, ...
Jesus, have mercy on all lay leaders, ...
Jesus, have mercy on priests who are sick, ...
Jesus, have mercy on all the elderly priests, ...
Jesus, have mercy on the dying priests, ...
Jesus, have mercy on the young priests, ...
Jesus, have mercy on priests who are weak, ...
Jesus, have mercy on priests who are lukewarm, ...
Jesus, have mercy on priests who are suffering, ...
Jesus, have mercy on priests who are being persecuted, ...
Jesus, have mercy on priests who are losing faith, ...
Jesus, have mercy on all the priests who instituted Sacraments to me, ...
Jesus, have mercy on the priest who baptized me, ...
Jesus, have mercy on all the priests who heard my confession, ...
Jesus, have mercy on the priest/Bishop who gave me the sacrament of confirmation, ...
Jesus, have mercy on my parish priest, ...
Glory be...

Scriptures to meditate

I sought among them for a man who might set up a hedge, and stand in the gap before me on behalf of the land, so that I might not destroy it; and I found no one. (Eze 22:30)

I fell prostrate before the Lord, just as before, for forty days and nights, not eating bread, and not drinking water, because of all your sins, which you had committed against the Lord, and because you provoked him to anger. For I feared his indignation and wrath, which had been stirred up against you, so that he was willing to destroy you. And the Lord heeded me at this time also. (Deut 9:18-19)

As for me, when they were sick, my clothing was sackcloth: I humbled my soul with fasting; and I prayed with head bowed on my bosom. I grieved myself as though he had been my friend or brother: I bowed down heavily, as one mourns for his mother. (Ps 35:13-14)

Be vigilant with every kind of earnest supplication, for all the saints. (Eph 6:18)

Pray at all times in spirit, and so be vigilant with every kind of earnest supplication, for all the saints, and also for me, so that words may be given to me, as I open my mouth with faith to make known the mystery of the Gospel. (Eph 6:18-19)

Peter was detained in prison. But prayers were being made without ceasing, by the Church, to God on his behalf. (Acts 12:5)

We give thanks to God, the Father of our Lord Jesus Christ, praying for you always. (Col 1:3)

I give thanks to God, whom I serve, as my forefathers did, with a pure conscience. For without ceasing I hold the remembrance of you in my prayers, night and day. (2 Tim 1:3)

We have not ceased praying for you and requesting that you be filled with the knowledge of his will, with all wisdom and spiritual understanding, so that you may walk in a manner worthy of God, being pleasing in all things, being fruitful in every good work, and increasing in the knowledge of God. (Col 1:10)

First of all, to make supplications, prayers, petitions, and thanksgivings for all men, for kings, and for all who are in high places, so that we may lead a quiet and tranquil life in all piety and chastity. (1 Tim 2:1-2)

Ministry and Evangelization

Prayer

Jesus fill me with your love,… *and use me for your kingdom*
Jesus fill me with your Holy Spirit,… *and use me for your kingdom*
Jesus fill me with compassion,… *and use me for your kingdom*
Jesus fill me with your truth,… *and use me for your kingdom*
Jesus fill me with your presence,… *and use me for your kingdom*
Jesus fill me with your Word,… *and use me for your kingdom*
Jesus fill me with your divine wisdom,… *and use me for your kingdom*
Jesus fill me with zeal for evangelization,… *and use me for your kingdom*
Jesus teach me your word,… *and use me for your kingdom*
Jesus fill me with your power,… *and use me for your kingdom*
Jesus give me thirst for souls,… *and use me for your kingdom*
Jesus fill me with the charisms of the Spirit,… *and use me for your kingdom*
Jesus fill me with faith,… *and use me for your kingdom*
Jesus make me holy,… *and use me for your kingdom*
Jesus give me boldness and strength *and use me for your kingdom*
Glory be…

Scriptures to meditate

With great power, the Apostles were rendering testimony to the Resurrection of Jesus Christ our Lord. And great grace was in them all. (Acts 4:33)

Do not be afraid. Instead, speak out and do not be silent. For I am with you. And no one will take hold of you, so as to do you harm. (Acts 18:9-10)

You shall go forth to everyone to whom I will send you. And you shall speak all that I will command you. (Jer 1:7)

Today I have appointed you over nations and over kingdoms, so that you may root up, and pull down, and destroy, and scatter, and so that you may build and plant. (Jer 1:10)

Amen, amen, I say to you, whoever believes in me shall also do the works that I do. And greater things than these shall he do, for I go to the Father. (Jn 14:12)

I have established you like a new threshing cart, having serrated blades. You will thresh the mountains and crush them. And you will turn the hills into chaff. (Is 41:15)

You are my war club, my weapon of battle: with you I smash nations; with you I destroy kingdoms; with you I smash the horse and its rider; with you I smash the chariot and the charioteer. (Jer 51:20-21)

Go on, therefore, and I will be in your mouth. And I will teach you what you shall say. (Exo 4:12)

You are a chosen generation, a royal priesthood, a holy nation, an acquired people, so that you may proclaim the mighty acts of him who has called you out of darkness into his marvelous light. (1 Pet 2:9)

Biblical Prayers

Abandonment (feelings of being abandoned)
O God, my God, Why have you forsaken me? Why are you so far from helping me, and from the words of my groaning? My God, I cry out by day, and you will not heed, and by night, but find no rest. (Ps 22:2-3)

Addictions (Substance addictions)
And now, what is it that awaits me? My hope is in you. Rescue me from all my iniquities. (Ps 39:7-8)

Addictions (Drug addiction)
O Lord, do not take your tender mercies far from me. Let Your mercy and your truth ever sustain me. For evils without number have surrounded me. My iniquities have taken hold of me, and I was not able to see. They have been multiplied beyond the hairs of my head. And my heart has forsaken me. (Ps 40:11-12)

May the groans of the shackled enter before you. According to the greatness of your arm, take possession of those doomed to die. (Ps 79:11)

Bible (Prayer before reading the Bible)
I am your servant. Give me understanding, so that I may know your decrees. (Ps 119:125)

Bible (Prayer after reading the Bible)
I rejoice at your word, as one that finds great spoil. I hate and abhor lying: but I love your law. (Ps 119:162-163)

Commandments (Prayer after examining the conscience using the Ten Commandments)
I meditated on your commandments, which I loved. And I lifted up my hands to your commandments, which I loved. (Ps 119:47-48)

Confession (Prayer after confession)
Create a clean heart in me, O God. And renew a right spirit within me. Do not cast me away from your presence; and do not take your Holy Spirit from me. Restore to me the joy of your salvation, and sustain in me a willing spirit. (Ps 51:11-13)

Confession *(Prayer of healing of the soul after confession)*
Lord, be merciful unto me: heal my soul; for I have sinned against you. (Ps 41:4)

Contentment *(Prayer to keep us content)*
Two things I have asked of you; do not deny them to me before I die. Remove, far from me, vanity and lying words. Give me neither begging, nor wealth. Apportion to me only the necessities of my life, lest perhaps, being filled, I might be enticed into denial, and say: 'Who is the Lord?' Or, being compelled by destitution, I might steal, and then perjure myself in the name of my God. (Pro 30:7-9)

Country *(Prayer for freedom if your country is ruled by another country)*
Save us, O God our savior! And gather us together, and rescue us from the nations, so that we may give thanks to your holy name, and may glory in your praise. (1 Chron 16:35)

Country *(Prayer for freedom from a wicked ruler (dictators))*
O Lord our God, save us from his hand, so that all the kingdoms of the earth may know that you alone are the Lord God. (2 Kgs 19:19)

And now, O Lord our God, save us from his hand. And let all the kingdoms of the earth acknowledge that you alone are Lord. (Is 37:20)

Death *(prayer before dying)*
Into your hands, I commend my spirit. You have redeemed me, O Lord, faithful God. (Ps 31:5)

Debt *(Prayer for freedom from financial debt)*
From the depths, I have cried out to you, O Lord. O Lord, hear my voice. Let your ears be attentive to the voice of my supplication. (Ps 130:1-2)

Deliverance
Rise up, O Lord, confront him and displace him. By your sword deliver my soul from the impious one. (Ps 17:13)

Drought
O God, you showered rain in plenty, whereby you restored your inheritance when it languished. Your people found a dwelling in it: you, O God have prepared, in your goodness, for the poor. (Ps 68:9-10)

Hear them from heaven, and forgive the sins of your servants and of your people. And reveal to them the good way, along which they should walk, and grant rain upon your land, which you have given to your people as a possession. (1 Kgs 8:36)

Employees (prayer over employees, maids, etc.)
O Lord, bless his substance, and receive the works of his hands. (Deut 33:11)

Eucharist (prayer before receiving communion)
Lord, I am not worthy that you should enter under my roof, but only say the word, and my servant shall be healed. (Matt 8:8)

Evangelization (prayer for evangelists to come and preach)
I beg you Lord, that the man of God, whom you sent, may come again, and may teach us what we ought to do. (Jdgs 13:8)

Evangelization (prayer asking God to use us)
Here I am. Send me. (Is 6:8)

Eyes (prayer for the purification of our eyes)
Lord, Father and God of my life. Do not leave me with the haughtiness of my eyes.(Sir 23:5)

Turn my eyes away, lest they see what is vain. Revive me in your way. (Ps 119:37)

Faith (prayer to increase our faith)
Lord, Increase our faith. (Luk 17:5)

Family (prayer for the healing of the family tree)
Do not remember against us the iniquities of our ancestors. May your mercies quickly meet us, for we have become exceedingly poor. (Ps 79:8)

Family blessing prayer
Bless the house of your servant, so that it may be forever before you. For you, O Lord God, have spoken. And so, let the house of your servant be blessed with your blessing forever. (2 Sam 7:29)

If only, when blessing, you will bless me, and will broaden my borders, and your hand will be with me, and you will keep me from hurt and harm. (1 Chron 4:10)

Fire (wild fire, forest fire)
To you, O Lord, I will cry out, because fire has devoured the beauty of the wilderness, and the flame has burned all the trees of the countryside. Yes, and even the beasts of the field cry out to you, like the dry ground thirsting for rain, because the fountains of waters have dried up, and fire has devoured the beauty of the wilderness. (Joel 1:19-20)

Fire (house fire)
The house of our sanctification and of our glory, where our ancestors praised you, has been completely consumed by fire, and all our admirable things have been turned into ruins. Should you restrain yourself, O Lord, concerning these things? Should you remain silent, and afflict us vehemently? (Is 64:11-12)

Flooding
Send forth your hand from on high: rescue me, and free me from the mighty waters. (Ps 144:7)

Flooding, drowning
Save me, O God; for the waters have come up to my neck. I sink in deep mire, where there is no standing: I am come into deep waters, where the floods overflow me. (Ps 69:1-2)

Forgiveness of sins
O God, be merciful to me, a sinner. (Luk 18:13)

O Lord, do not rebuke me in your fury, nor chastise me in your wrath. For your arrows have been driven into me, and your hand has been confirmed over me. (Ps 38:1-2)

Lord God, forgive, I beg you. (Amos 7:2)

Forgiveness of mortal sins
For your name's sake, O Lord, pardon my sin, for it is great. (Ps 25:11)

Friendships (Prayer for protection from bad company)
Do not turn aside my heart to words of evil, to making excuses for sins, with men who work iniquity; and I will not communicate, and let me not eat of their delicacies. (Ps 141:4)

Gluttony (Prayer for freedom from gluttony)
Lord, Father and God of my life. Do not leave me with the haughtiness of my eyes. And avert all evil desires from me. Let neither gluttony nor

sexual desire take hold of me, and do not give me over to shameless passion. (Sir 23:5-6)

Guilt (Prayer to free oneself from guilt)
I have sinned exceedingly in doing this. I beg you take away the guilt of your servant. For I have acted unwisely. (1 Chron 21:8)

Hatred (prayer when we are hated by people)
Have mercy upon me, O Lord; see my trouble which I suffer of them that hate me You have lifted me up from the gates of death, so that I may announce all your praises. (Ps 9:13)

Healing
Heal me, O Lord, and I will be healed. Save me, and I will be saved. For you are my praise. (Jer 17:14)

Healing prayer for incurable diseases (terminal sickness)
Let me live and I will praise you, and let your ordinances assist me. (Ps 119:175)

Your hands have made me and formed me all around, and, in this way, do you suddenly throw me away? Remember that you have fashioned me like clay; and will you reduce me to dust? Have you not extracted me like milk and curdled me like cheese? You have clothed me with skin and flesh. You have put me together with bones and nerves. You have assigned to me life and mercy, and your visitation has preserved my spirit. (Job 10:8-12)

Turn to me, Lord, and save my life. Save me for the sake of your steadfast love. For there is no one in death who would be mindful of you. And who will praise to you in sheol? (Ps 6:4-5)

Healing prayer for skin diseases (Leprosy, Eczema, etc.)
Lord, if you are willing, you can cleanse me. (Matt 8:2)

Healing prayer for physical pain
Have mercy on me, Lord, for I am languishing. Heal me, Lord, for my bones have become disturbed, and my soul has been very troubled. But as for you, Lord, how long? (Ps 6:2-3)

Healing prayer for blindness
Consider and hear me, O Lord my God: lighten my eyes, or I will sleep the sleep of death. (Ps 13:3)

Lord, let me see again. (Luk 18:41)

Healing prayer for our emotions
I have been altogether afflicted, Lord. Revive me according to your word. (Ps 119:107)

But as for you, Lord, O Lord: act on my behalf for your name's sake. For your mercy is sweet. Free me, for I am destitute and poor, and my heart has been disquieted within me. (Ps 109:21-22)

Idol worship
Could any of the graven images of the Gentiles send rain? Or are the heavens able to give showers? Have we not hoped in you, the Lord our God? For you have made all these things. (Jer 14:22)

Leader (prayer of a leader, politician, people in authority)
Give to your servant an understanding heart, so that he may be able to govern your people, and to discern between good and evil. For who will be able to govern this people, your people, who are so many? (1 Kgs 3:9)

Give to me wisdom and understanding, so that I may enter and depart before your people. For who is able worthily to judge this, your people, who are so great?" (2 Chron 1:10)

Lonliness
Look upon me and have mercy on me; for I am lonely and afflicted. The troubles of my heart have been multiplied. bring me out of my distress. (Ps 25:16-17)

Lying (prayer For freedom from the habit of lying)
Deliver me, O Lord, from lying lips, from a deceitful tongue. (Ps 120:2)

Marriage (prayer when choosing a life partner)
May you, O Lord, who knows the heart of everyone, reveal which one you have chosen. (Acts 1:24)

Masturbation
Avert all evil desires from me. Let neither gluttony nor sexual desire take hold of me, and do not give me over to shameless passion. (Sir 23:6)

Meal (Prayer of thanksgiving before meal)
It is he who remembered us in our low estate: for his steadfast love endures forever: And has redeemed us from our enemies: for his

steadfast love endures forever. Who gives food to all flesh: for his steadfast love endures forever. O give thanks unto the God of heaven: for his steadfast love endures forever. (Ps 136:23-26)

Mercy (prayer for God's mercy)

You are a gracious God, and merciful, slow to anger, and of great kindness, and ready to forgive. (Jon 4:2)

Gaze down from heaven, and behold from your holy habitation and from your glory. Where is your zeal, and your strength, the fullness of your heart and of your compassion? They have held themselves back from me. (Is 63:15)

Ministry (prayer of God's servants)

Let your face shine on your servant; save me in your unfailing love. (Ps 31:16)

O Lord, God of Abraham, and Isaac, and Israel, reveal this day that you are the God of Israel, and that I am your servant, and that I have acted, in all these things, in accord with your precept. (1 Kgs 18:36)

Money and Finances

Oh that you would bless me, and will broaden my borders, and your hand will be with me, and you will keep me from hurt and harm. (1 Chron 4:10)

Morning prayer for direction

Make me hear your steadfast love in the morning. For I have hoped in you. Make known to me the way that I should walk. For I have lifted up my soul to you. (Ps 143:8)

Morning prayer before worship and singing praises

My heart is steadfast, O God, my heart is steadfast. I will sing, and I will make melody. Rise up, my soul. Rise up, psaltery and harp. I will arise in early morning. I will give thanks to you, O Lord, among the peoples. I will give praises to you among the nations. (Ps 57:7-10)

Old age

Cast me not off in the time of old age; forsake me not when my strength fails. (Ps 71:9)

Now also when I am old and with grey hairs, O God, forsake me not; until I have proclaimed your strength unto this generation, and your power to everyone that is to come. (Ps 71:18)

Orphans
For you are our Father, and Abraham has not known us, and Israel has been ignorant of us. You are our Father, O Lord our Redeemer. (Is 63:16)

Parents
Grant my child a perfect heart, so that he may keep your commandments, your decrees, and your statutes, and so that he may accomplish all things. (1 chron 29:19)

Pornogaphy
Turn my eyes away, lest they see what is vain. Revive me in your way. (Ps 119:37)

Prayer (Closing prayer)
Let the words of my mouth, and the meditation of my heart, be acceptable in your sight, O Lord, my strength, and my redeemer. (Ps 19:14)

Pregnancy and labor
Look down upon me and have mercy on me. Grant your strength to your servant, and save the child of your handmaid. (Ps 86:16)

Presence of God
We follow you wholeheartedly, and we fear you, and we seek your presence. Do not put us to shame, but deal with us in agreement with your patience and according to the multitude of your mercies. (Dan 3:41-42)

Priest's prayer for his parish
Look with favor upon the prayer of your servant and upon his petitions, O Lord, my God. Listen to the cry and the prayer, which your servant prays before you this day, so that your eyes may be open over this house, night and day, over the house about which you said, 'My name shall be there,' so that you may heed the prayer that your servant is praying in this place to you. (1 Kgs 8:28-29)

Protection
Protect me, O Lord, because I have hoped in you. (Ps 16:1)

Rebellion

See, O Lord, that I am in tribulation. My stomach has been disturbed, my heart has been subverted within me, for I am very rebellious. (Lam 1:20)

Refugees

Save us, O Lord our God, and gather us from the nations, so that we may give thanks to your holy name and glory in your praise. (Ps 106:47)

Repentance

O God, be merciful to me, a sinner. (Luk 18:13)

Restitution and reparation (prayer for God's mercy on those who are victims of our sin)

It is I who sinned; it is I who did evil. This flock, what does it deserve? But let not your people be struck down. (1 Chron 21:17)

Sinner (Sinner's prayer)

O Lord, though our iniquities testify against us, act Lord, for your name's sake: for our backslidings are many; we have sinned against you. (Jer 14:7)

And now, O Lord, you are our Father, yet truly, we are clay. And you are our Maker, and we are all the works of your hands. Do not be so angry, O Lord, and no longer call to mind our iniquity. Behold, consider that we are all your people. (Is 64:8-9)

Sexual sins

Help us, O God, our Savior. And free us, Lord, for the glory of your name. And forgive us our sins for the sake of your name. (Ps 79:9)

Speech (Prayer for control over speech)

O Lord, set a guard over my mouth and a door enclosing my lips. (Ps 141:3)

Storm, Hurricane, Monsoon, Thunderstorm

Be merciful to me, O God, be merciful to me. For my soul trusts in you. And I will hope in the shadow of your wings, until the storms passes away. (Ps 57:1)

Suicidal thoughts

I cried to you, O Lord; and to the Lord I made supplication. What profit is there in my blood, when I go down to the pit? Shall the dust praise you?

shall it declare your truth? Hear, O Lord, and have mercy on me: Lord, be my helper. (Ps 30:8-10)

Surgery (Prayer of thanksgiving after surgery or healing from any sickness)

O Lord my God, I cried to you for help, and you have healed me. O Lord, you brought up my soul from Sheol, restored me to life from among those gone down to the Pit. (Ps 30:1-2)

Surrender

My Father, if it is possible, let this chalice pass away from me. Yet truly, let it not be as I will, but as you will. (Matt 26:39)

Behold, I am the handmaid of the Lord. Let it be done to me according to your word. (Luk 1:38)

Thanksgiving prayer for the gift of family

Who am I, O Lord God, and what is my house, that you would bring me to this point? (2 Sam 7:18)

Thanksgiving prayer for protection

I will give thanks to you, O Lord, O King, and I will praise you, O God my Savior. I will give thanks to your name: for you have been a helper and protector to me. (Sir 51:1-2)

Thanksgiving prayer after a miracle or blessing

Father, I thank you that you have heard me. And I know that you hear me always: (Jn 11:41-42)

Tithing prayer

I bring the first of the fruit of the ground that you, O Lord, have given me. (Deut 26:10)

I know, my God, that you test hearts, and that you love uprightness. Therefore, in the uprightness of my heart, I also have offered all these things willingly. (1 Chron 29:17)

Understanding (prayer for the gift of understanding)

Your hands have created me and formed me. Give me understanding, and I will learn your commandments. (Ps 119:73)

God's Promises

Abandoned
I will not abandon you, and I will not neglect you. (Heb 13:5)

Addictions
Sin will not have dominion over you. For you are not under the law, but under grace. (Rom 6:14)

Almsgiving
Give liberally and without grieving when you give: because for on this account the Lord your God shall bless you in all your works, and in all that you put your hand into. (Deut 15:10)

Angelic Protection
Behold, I will send my Angel, who will go before you, and preserve you on your journey, and lead you into the place that I have prepared. (Exo 23:20)

Anxiety
Cast all your anxiety upon him, for he takes care of you. (1 Pet 5:7)

Baptism
You have been washed, you have been sanctified, and you have been justified: all in the name of our Lord Jesus Christ and in the Spirit of our God. (1 Cor 6:11)

Bible (Word of God)
All flesh is like the grass and all its glory is like the flower of the grass. The grass withers and its flower falls away. But the Word of the Lord endures for eternity. (1 Pet 1:24)

Blood of Christ
If we walk in the light, just as he also is in the light, then we have fellowship with one another, and the blood of Jesus Christ, his Son, cleanses us from all sin. (1 Jn 1:7)

Body
Do you not know that your bodies are the Temple of the Holy Spirit, who is in you, whom you have from God, and that you are not your own? For

you have been bought at a great price. Glorify and carry God in your body. (1 Cor 6:19-20)

Born again
We know that everyone who is born of God does not sin. Instead, the one who was born of God protects him, and the evil one cannot touch him. (1 Jn 5:18)

Brokenhearted (Heartbroken)
He heals the brokenhearted and binds up their wounds. (Ps 147:3)

Career
I know the plans that I have for you, says the Lord, plans of your welfare, and not for evil, to give you a future of hope. (Jer 29:11)

Charisms of the Holy Spirit
The manifestation of the Spirit is given to each one toward what is beneficial. Certainly, to one, through the Spirit, is given words of wisdom; but to another, according to the same Spirit, words of knowledge; to another, in the same Spirit, faith; to another, in the one Spirit, the gift of healing; to another, miraculous works; to another, prophecy; to another, the discernment of spirits; to another, different kinds of tongues; to another, the interpretation of tongues. (1 Cor 12:7-10)

Childless couples
He gives the barren woman to live in a house, makes her the joyful mother of children. (Ps 113:9)

Church
I say to you, that you are Peter, and upon this rock I will build my Church, and the gates of Hell shall not prevail against it. (Matt 16:18)

Death (fear of death)
Do not be afraid of those who kill the body, but are not able to kill the soul. But instead fear him who is able to destroy both soul and body in Hell. (Matt 10:28)

Depression
Take off, O Jerusalem, the garment of your sorrow and affliction, and put on your beauty and the honor of that eternal glory, which you have from God. God will surround you with a double garment of righteousness, and he will set a crown on your head of everlasting honor. (Bar 5:1-2)

Desires (good desires)
Delight in the Lord, and he will grant to you the desires of your heart. (Ps 37:4)

Despair
We are afflicted on every side, yet not distressed; we are perplexed, but not in despair; Persecuted, but not forsaken; cast down, but not destroyed; Always carrying in the body the death of our Lord Jesus, so that the life also of Jesus might be made visible in our body. (2 Cor 4:8-10)

Desperate, Desperation
My soul waits in silence for God alone? For from him is my salvation. Yes, he alone is my rock and my salvation. He is my fortress; I will never be moved. Yet, truly, My soul waits for God alone. For from him is my hope. For he is my rock and my Savior. He is my fortress; I will not be moved. In God is my salvation and my glory. He is the God of my help, and my hope is in God. (Ps 62:1-2,5-7)

Direction and counsel, decision making
I will instruct you and teach you in the way which you should go: I will guide you with my eyes upon you. (Ps 32:8)

Trust in the Lord with all your heart, and do not depend upon your own insight. In all your ways, acknowledge him, and he himself will direct your steps. (Pro 3:5-6)

Disability
I am the Lord your God. I hold you by your right hand, and I say to you: Do not be afraid. I will help you. (Is 41:13)

Disaster, natural calamity, trauma
Do not fear unexpected terror, nor the power of the impious falling upon you. For the Lord will be at your side, and he will guard your feet, so that you may not be seized. (Pro 3:25-26)

Discouragement
Be strong and courageous; be not afraid, neither be dismayed: for the Lord your God is with you wherever you go. (Josh 1:9)

Distraction

You will keep him in perfect peace, whose mind is stayed on you: because he trusts in you. (Is 26:2)

Distress

This is my comfort in my distress: for your promises gives me life. (Ps 119:50)

Dizzyness

It is he that gives power to the weary, and strengthens them that are powerless. Youths shall faint, and labor, and young men shall fall exhausted. But they that hope in the Lord shall renew their strength, they shall take wings as eagles, they shall run and not be weary, they shall walk and not faint. (Is 40:29-31)

Driving (fear of driving)

Your justifier shall go before you, the glory of the Lord shall be your rear guard. (Is 58:8-9)

Education (God's promise for parents about their children's education)

All your children will be taught by the Lord. And great will be the prosperity of your children. (Is 54:13)

Enemies

What should we say about these things? If God is for us, who is against us? (Rom 8:31)

When the ways of man will please the Lord, even his enemies will be at peace with him. (Pro 16:7)

Eucharist (Holy Mass)

I am the living bread, who descended from heaven. If anyone eats from this bread, he shall live forever. (Jn 6:51)

Eucharistic Adoration

Come to me, all you who labor and have been burdened, and I will give you rest. (Matt 11:28)

Evangelization

Everyone who acknowledges me before men, I also will acknowledge before my Father, who is in heaven. But whoever will have denied me before men, I also will deny before my Father, who is in heaven. (Matt 10:32-33)

Evil Spirits (Demons)
Behold, I have given you authority to tread upon serpents and scorpions, and upon all the powers of the enemy, and nothing shall hurt you. (Luk 10:19)

Examination of conscience
You also are saved, in a similar manner, by baptism, not by the testimony of sordid flesh, but by the examination of a good conscience in God, through the resurrection of Jesus Christ. (1 Pet 3:21)

Failure
Do not be afraid, and do not dread or have fear of them. For the Lord your God himself goes with you, and he will neither fail you nor abandon you. (Deut 31:6)

Faith
All things whatsoever that you shall ask for in prayer with faith, you shall receive. (Matt 21:22)

Family prayer
Again I say to you, that if two of you have agreed on earth, about anything whatsoever that you have requested, it shall be done for you by my Father, who is in heaven. For wherever two or three are gathered in my name, there am I, in their midst. (Matt 18:19-20)

Farmers, business people, self employed
Those who sow in tears shall reap with shouts of joy. When departing, they went forth and wept, sowing their seeds. But when returning, they will arrive with shouts of joy, carrying their sheaves. (Ps 126:5-6)

Fasting
He who observes the day, observes for the Lord. And he who eats, eats for the Lord; for he gives thanks to God. And he who does not eat, does not eat for the Lord, and he gives thanks to God. (Rom 14:6)

Fear
Do not fear, for I am with you. Do not be afraid, for I am your God. I will strengthen you, and I will help you, and with my victorious right hand, I will uphold you. (Is 41:10)

Fear of God

Happy is everyone who fears the Lord; who walks in his ways. For you shall eat the labor of your hands: happy shall you be, and it shall be well with you. Your wife shall be as a fruitful vine within your house: your children like be like olive plants around your table. Behold, thus shall the man be blessed who fears the Lord. (Ps 128:1-4)

Fear of people

The Lord is my light and my salvation, whom shall I fear? The Lord is the stronghold of my life, of whom shall I be afraid? (Ps 27:1)

Ghosts (fear of ghosts and darkness)

Little children, you are of God, and so you have conquered him. For he who is in you is greater than he who is in the world. (1 Jn 4:4)

Forgiveness

If you will forgive men their sins, your heavenly Father also will forgive you your offenses. But if you will not forgive men, neither will your Father forgive you your sins. (Matt 6:14-15)

Forgiveness of sins

I am. I am the very One who wipes away your iniquities for my own sake. And I will not remember your sins. (Is 43:25)

Freedom, Freewill

For you, have been called to freedom. Only you must not make freedom into an occasion for the flesh, but instead, serve one another through love. (Gal 5:13)

Fruits of the Holy Spirit

Whoever has received the seed into good soil, this is he who hears the word, and understands it, and so he bears fruit, and he produces: some a hundred fold, and another sixty fold, and another thirty fold. (Matt 13:23)

Future

I know the plans that I have for you, said the Lord, plans for your welfare, and not for evil, to give you a future of hope. (Jer 29:11)

Gift of Tongues

These signs will accompany those who believe. In my name, they shall cast out demons. They will speak in new languages. (Mrk 16:17)

God's Love
For the mountains will be moved, and the hills be removed. But my steadfast love will not depart from you.(Is 54:10)

Grace
For by grace, you have been saved through faith. And this is not your doing, for it is a gift of God. (Eph 2:8)

Guilt
Let us draw near with a true heart, in the fullness of faith, having hearts cleansed from an evil conscience, and bodies absolved with clean water. Let us hold fast to the confession of our hope, without wavering, for he who has promised is faithful. (Heb 10:22-23)

Hard heartedness
I will give them one heart. And I will put a new spirit within them. And I will take away the heart of stone from their flesh. And I will give them a heart of flesh. (Eze 11:19)

Healing
He himself was wounded because of our iniquities. He was bruised because of our wickedness. The discipline of our peace was upon him. And by his wounds, we are healed. (Is 53:5)

Heaven
In my Father's house, there are many dwelling places. If there were not so, would I have told you that I go to prepare a place for you. And if I go and prepare a place for you, I will return again, and then I will take you to myself, so that where I am, you also may be. (Jn 14:2-3)

Holy Spirit
After this, it will happen that I will pour out my spirit upon all flesh, and your sons and your daughters will prophesy; your elders will dream dreams, and your youths will see visions. Moreover, in those days I will pour out my spirit upon my servants and handmaids. (Joel 2:28-29)

Homeless
God gives the solitary a home to live in. he brings out those who are bound with chains to prosperity. (Ps 68:6)

Humility
Be humbled in the sight of the Lord, and he will exalt you. (Jas 4:10)

Hunger and Thirst

He has satisfied the thirsty, and he has satisfied the hungry soul with good things. (Ps 107:9)

Insults, ridicule, and persecution by people

Do not be afraid of disgrace among men, and do not dread when they revile you. For the worm will consume them like a garment, and the moth will devour them like wool. But my deliverance will be forever, and my salvation will be from generation to generation. (Is 51:7-8)

Jesus

God so loved the world that he gave his only-begotten Son, so that all who believe in him may not perish, but may have eternal life. (Jn 3:16)

Joy

I will rejoice greatly in the Lord, and my soul will exult in my God. For he has clothed me with the vestments of salvation, and he has wrapped me in the clothing of justice, like a groom arrayed with a crown, and like a bride adorned with her jewels. (Is 61:10)

Kindness

A kind man benefits his own soul. But whoever is cruel harms himself. (Pro 11:17)

Kingdom of God

Seek first the kingdom of God and his righteousness, and all these things shall be added to you as well. (Matt 6:33)

Lawsuits (faced with court case)

No weapon which has been formed to use against you will succeed. And every tongue that shall rise against you in judgment, you shall resist. (Is 54:17)

Lonliness

Behold, I am with you always, even to the end of age. (Matt 28:20)

Lord's day

They will keep my Sabbaths, and they will choose the things that I will, and they will hold to my covenant. I will give them a place in my house, within my walls, and a name better than sons and daughters. I will give them an everlasting name, which will never perish. (Is 56:4-5)

Loss of job, Loss of savings, economic downfall
Behold, God is my savior, I will trust, and I will not be afraid. For the Lord is my strength and my might, and he has become my salvation. (Is 12:2)

Love for God
We know that all things work together unto good, for those who love God, who are called in accordance with his purpose. (Rom 8:28)

Love for neighbor
Whoever loves his brother abides in the light, and there is no cause of offense in him. But whoever hates his brother is in the darkness, and in darkness he walks, and he does not know where he is going. For the darkness has blinded his eyes. (1 Jn 2:10-11)

Marriage
Male and female, he created them. And God blessed them, and he said, "Increase and multiply." (Gen 1:27-28)

Money and finances
My God shall supply all your needs according to his riches in glory by Christ Jesus. (Phil 4:19)

Mother Mary
When Jesus had seen his mother and the disciple whom he loved standing near, he said to his mother, "Woman, behold your son." Next, he said to the disciple, "Behold your mother." And from that hour, the disciple accepted her as his own. (Jn 19:26-27)

Memories (bad)
Do not call to mind the former things, nor consider the things of old. Behold, I am accomplishing new things. And now, it will spring forth. With certainty, you will know them. I will make a way in the wilderness, and rivers in the desert. (Is 43:18-19)

Music (Christian)
Whenever the evil spirit from the Lord assailed Saul, David took up his stringed instrument, and he struck it with his hand, and Saul was refreshed and uplifted. For the evil spirit withdrew from him. (1 Sam 16:23)

Nightmares
When you sleep, you shall not fear. When you rest, your sleep also will be sweet. (Pro 3:24)

Obedience to God
If we obey God, and withdraw from all sin, and do what is good, he will be pleased with us and make us prosperous. (Tob 4:21)

Old age
And even to your old age I am he; and even with your hairs will I carry you: I have made, and I will bear; even I will carry, and will deliver you. (Is 46:4)

Oppression
The Lord is a refuge for the oppressed, a stronghold in times of tribulation. (Ps 9:9)

Orphans
If my father and my mother forsake me, the Lord will take me up. (Ps 27:10)

Pain
May you be strengthened with all the might that comes from his glorious power, and may you be prepared to endure everything with patience and longsuffering, while joyfully giving thanks to the Father, who has enabled you to partake in the inheritance of the saints in the light. (Col 1:11-12)

Parents (Promise for the children who are away from the Lord))
Behold, your children approach, whom you sent away scattered. They approach, gathering together, from the east all the way to the west, at the word of the Holy One, rejoicing in the honor of God. (Bar 4:37)

Parents (God's promise for our children who are lost to sin and addictions)
I will strengthen the house of Judah, and I will save the house of Joseph, and I will convert them, because I will have mercy on them. And they will be as they were when I had not cast them away. For I am the Lord their God, and I will hear them. (Zech 10:6)

Parents (God's promise of the Holy Spirit upon our children)
I will pour out waters upon the thirsty ground, and rivers upon the dry land. I will pour out my Spirit upon your descendants, and my blessing upon your offspring. (Is 44:3)

Parents (God's promise for lost and missing children)
They will return from the land of the enemy. And there is hope for your very end, says the Lord. And your children will return to their own land. (Jer 31:16-17)

Parents (God's promise for children who are unbelievers)
Even the captives will be taken away from the strong, even what has been taken by the powerful will be saved. And truly, I will contend with those who contend with you, and I will save your children. (Is 49:25)

Patience
I have waited patiently for the Lord, and he was attentive to me. And he heard my prayers and he led me out of the pit of misery and the miry bog.(Ps 40:1)

Peace
Peace I leave for you; my Peace I give to you. Not in the way that the world gives, do I give to you. Do not let your heart be troubled, and let it not fear. (Jn 14:27)

Persecution
Blessed are those who endure persecution for the sake of righteousness, for theirs is the kingdom of heaven. (Matt 5:10)

Poverty
Blessed are you poor, for yours is the kingdom of God. Blessed are you who are hungry now, for you shall be satisfied. Blessed are you who are weeping now, for you shall laugh. (Luk 6:20-21)

Prayer
When you seek me, you will find me; if you have sought me with your whole heart, I will be found by you, says the Lord. And I will restore your fortunes and gather you from all the nations where I have driven you. (Jer 29:13-14)

Rejection
You, O Israel, are my servant, O Jacob, whom I have chosen, the offspring of my friend Abraham. For his sake, I have taken you from the ends of the earth, and I have called you from its distant places. And I said to you: "You are my servant. I have chosen you, and I have not cast you aside." (Is 41:8-9)

Self denial
Anyone who has left behind home, or brothers, or sisters, or father, or mother, or wife, or children, or land, for the sake of my name, shall receive one hundred times more, and shall possess eternal life. But many of those who are first shall be last, and the last shall be first. (Matt 19:29-30)

Self Esteem, low self self esteem
Before I formed you in the womb, I knew you. And before you went forth from the womb, I sanctified you. And I made you a prophet to the nations. (Jer 1:5)

Shame and embarrassment
The Lord God is my helper. Therefore, I have not been disgraced. Therefore, I have set my face like a very hard rock, and I know that I will not be put to shame. (Is 50:7)

Shyness, timidity
God has not given us a spirit of cowardice, but of power, and of love, and of a sound mind. (2 Tim 1:7)

Sleep, sleeplessness, insomnia
I will sleep and I will rest in peace. For you, O Lord, make me lie down in safety. (Ps 4:8)

Sorrow, Sadness
They will approach with weeping. And I will lead them back with consolations. And I will lead them through the torrents of water, by an upright way, and they will not stumble in it. For I have become Father to Israel, and Ephraim is my firstborn. (Jer 31:9)

Strength
I can do all things in him who strengthens me. (Phil 4:13)

Stress

Come to me, all you who labor and have been burdened, and I will give you rest. Take my yoke upon you, and learn from me, for I am meek and humble of heart; and you shall find rest for your souls. For my yoke is easy and my burden is light. (Matt 11:28-30)

Suffering

We know that all things work together unto good, for those who love God, who are called in accordance with his purpose. (Rom 8:28)

Suicidal thoughts

I shall not die, but live, and declare the works of the Lord. (Ps 118:17)

Talents

Whether you eat or drink, or whatever else you may do, do everything for the glory of God. (1 Cor 10:31)

Tears

Bitterly, you will not weep. Mercifully, he will take pity on you. At the voice of your outcry, as soon as he hears, he will respond to you. (Is 30:19)

Temptations

No temptation has overtaken you such as is not common to everyone: but God is faithful, who will not let you be tested beyond what you are able; but with the temptation he will also make a way to escape, so that you may be able to endure it. (1 Cor 10:13)

Tithing

Bring all the tithes into the storehouse, and let there be food in my house. And test me about this, says the Lord, as to whether I will not open to you the floodgates of heaven, and pour out to you a blessing, all the way to abundance. And I will rebuke for your sakes the devourer, and he will not corrupt the fruit of your land. Neither will the vine in the field be barren, says the Lord of hosts. (Mal 3:10-11)

Tiredness

I will satisfy the weary, and I will replenish all who are faint. Therefore I awoke, and looked; and my sleep was pleasant unto me. (Jer 31:25-26)

Thoughts (troubled thoughts, disturbing thoughts, obsessive thoughts)

The peace of God, which surpasses all understanding, shall keep your hearts and minds through Christ Jesus. (Phil 4:7)

Thoughts (Sexual thoughts)

In all things, take up the shield of faith, with which you may be able to extinguish all the fiery darts of the most wicked one. (Eph 6:16)

Troubled in spirit, Trials, Troubles, Tribulations

The Lord is near to those who are troubled in heart, and he will save the crushed in spirit. (Ps 34:18)

Wait on God

The Lord is good to those who wait on him, to the soul that seeks him. It is good to stand ready in silence for the salvation of God. (Lam 3:25-26)

War

They will make war against you, but they will not prevail. For I am with you, says the Lord, so that I may deliver you. (Jer 1:19)

Will of God

The world is passing away, with its desire. But whoever does the will of God abides unto eternity. (1 Jn 2:17)

Wisdom

If anyone among you is in need of wisdom, let him ask God, who gives abundantly to all without reproach, and it shall be given to him. (Jas 1:5)

God's Warning about Sin and Evil

Abortion

For three wicked deeds of the sons of Ammon, and for four, I will not turn away the punishment, in so far as he has cut up the pregnant women of Gilead, so as to expand his limits. (Amos 1:13)

Adultery

Whoever is an adulterer, because of the emptiness of his heart, will destroy his own soul. He gathers shame and dishonor to himself, and his disgrace will not be wiped away. (Pro 6:32-33)

Alcoholism

Do not gaze into wine when it turns gold, when its color shines in the glass. It enters pleasantly, but in the end, it will bite like a snake, and it will spread poison like a king of snakes. (Pro 23:31-32)

Anger

Cease from anger, and forsake rage; have no emulation to do evil; it brings only harm. (Ps 37:8)

Arrogance

Talk no more so proudly; let not arrogance come out of your mouth: for the Lord is a God of knowledge, and by him actions are weighed. (1 Sam 2:3)

Atheism

The fool has said in his heart, "There is no God." They are corrupt, and they do abominable deeds. There is no one who does good; there is not even one. (Ps 14:1)

Bitterness

See to it that no one fails to obtain the grace of God, lest any root of bitterness spring up and impede you, and by it, many might be defiled. (Heb 12:15)

Blasphemy

Jerusalem is ruined, and Judah has fallen, because their words and their plans are against the Lord, in order to provoke the eyes of his majesty. (Is 3:8)

Boasting

What is your life? It is a mist that appears for a brief time, and afterwards will vanish away. So what you ought to say is: "If the Lord wills," or, "If we live," we will do this or that. But now you exult in your arrogance. All such boasting is wicked. (Jas 4:15-16)

Bribe

Neither shall you accept bribes, which blind even the prudent and subvert the words of the just. (Exo 23:8)

Cheating

Woe to one who builds his house with injustice and his upper rooms without judgment, who oppresses his friend without cause and does not pay him his wages. (Jer 22:13)

Complaining

Brothers, do not complain against one another, so that you may not be judged. Behold, the judge stands before the door. (Jas 5:9)

Cursing

No man is able to rule over the tongue, a restless evil, full of deadly poison. By it we bless God the Father, and by it we speak evil of men, who have been made in the likeness of God. From the same mouth proceeds blessing and cursing. My brothers, these things ought not to be so! (Jas 3:8-10)

Discontentment

There is great gain in Godliness with contentment. For we brought nothing into this world, and there is no doubt that we can take nothing away. But, if we have food and some kind of covering, we will be content with these. (1 Tim 6:6-8)

Dishonesty in business

Do not choose to be anxious for dishonest wealth. For these things will not benefit you in the day of darkness and retribution. (Sir 5:8)

Divorce
Take heed to your spirit, and let none deal treacherously against the wife of his youth. For the Lord, the God of Israel, says that he hates divorce. (Mal 2:15-16)

Doubt
He who doubts is like a wave on the ocean, which is moved about by the wind and carried away; then a man should not consider that he would receive anything from the Lord. For a man who is double-minded is unstable in all his ways. (Jas 1:6-8)

Drug Addiction
Do not court death by the error of your life, nor procure your destruction by the works of your hands. (Wis 1:12)

Envy
When your enemy will fall, do not be glad, and do not let your heart exult in his ruin. (Pro 24:17)

Fornication
Flee from fornication. Every sin whatsoever that a man commits is outside of the body, but whoever fornicates, sins against his own body. (1 Cor 6:18)

Gambling
When an inheritance is obtained hastily in the beginning, in the end it will be without a blessing. (Pro 20:21)

Gluttony
Whether you eat or drink, or whatever else you may do, do everything for the glory of God. (1 Cor 10:31)

Gossip
Whoever hates gossip extinguishes evil. (Sir 19:6)

Greed
Watch out and guard yourselves from every kind of greed; for a person's life is not found in the abundance of the things that he possesses. (Luk 12:15)

Hatred
If anyone says that he loves God, but hates his brother, then he is a liar. For he who does not love his brother, whom he does see, in what way can he love God, whom he does not see? (1 Jn 4:20)

Haughtiness
The heart of a man is haughty before it is crushed and humbled before it is glorified. (Pro 18:12)

Homosexuality
You shall not commit sexual acts with a male, in place of sexual intercourse with a female, for this is an abomination. (Lev 18:22)

Incest
No man shall approach her who is a close blood-relative to him, so as to uncover her nakedness. I am the Lord. (Lev 18:6)

Jealousy
For where there is jealousy and selfish ambition, there will be disorder and every vile practice. (Jas 3:16)

Judging
Do not judge, so that you may not be judged. For with whatever judgment you judge, so shall you be judged; and with whatever measure you measure out, so shall it be measured back to you. (Matt 7:1-2)

Laziness
The intentions of the robust continually bring forth abundance. But all the lazy are continually in need. (Pro 21:5)

Lust
Let us not indulge in sexual immorality, as some of them did, and so twenty three thousand fell on one day. And let us not test Christ, as some of them did, and so they perished by serpents. (1 Cor 10:8-9)

Lying
The bread of lies is sweet to a man. But afterwards, his mouth will be filled with pebbles. (Pro 20:17)

Masturbation
If your right eye causes you to sin, root it out and cast it away from you. For it is better for you that one of your members perish, than that your whole body be cast into Hell. And if your right hand causes you to sin,

cut it off and cast it away from you. For it is better for you that one of your members perish, than that your whole body go into Hell. (Matt 5:29-30)

Mocking others

Whoever mocks the poor rebukes his Maker. And whoever rejoices in the ruin of another will not go unpunished. (Pro 17:5)

Money (love of money)

Keep your lives free from the love of money; be content with what you have. For he himself has said, "I will not leave you, and I will not abandon you." (Heb 13:5)

Murder

Envy, murder, inebriation, carousing, and similar things. About these things, I continue to preach to you, as I have preached to you: that those who act in this way shall not obtain the kingdom of God. (Gal 5:21)

Occult

Do not turn aside to astrologers, nor consult with soothsayers, so as to be polluted through them. I am the Lord your God. (Lev 19:31)

Porn

I say to you, that anyone who will have looked at a woman, so as to lust after her, has already committed adultery with her in his heart. (Matt 5:28)

Pride

Everyone who exalts himself shall be humbled, and whoever humbles himself shall be exalted. (Luk 14:11)

Procrastination

See to it that you live carefully, not like the foolish, but like the wise: making the most of the time, because the days are evil. (Eph 5:15-16)

Prostitution

Do you not know that your bodies are a part of Christ? So then, should I take a part of Christ and make it a part of a prostitute? Let it not be so! And do you not know that whoever is joined to a prostitute becomes one body? "For the two," he said, "shall be as one flesh." (1 Cor 6:15-16)

Quick temper, short temper
Do not be quickly moved to anger. For anger resides in the bosom of the foolish. (Eccl 7:9)

Racism
There is no distinction between Jew and Greek. For the same Lord is Lord over all, and is generous to all who call upon him. For all those who have called upon the name of the Lord shall be saved. (Rom 10:12)

Revenge
Do not seek revenge, neither should you be mindful of the injury of your fellow citizens. You shall love your friend as yourself. I am the Lord. (Lev 19:18)

Self exaltation
Do not appear glorious before the king, and do not stand in the place of the great. For it is better that it should be said to you, "Ascend to here," than that you should be humbled before the prince. (Pro 25:6-7)

Self-glory
If I glorify myself, my glory is nothing. It is my Father who glorifies me. (Jn 8:54)

Selfishness
For where there is jealousy and selfish ambition, there will be disorder and every vile practice. (Jas 3:16)

Self-importance
I say, through the grace that has been given to me, to all who are among you: not to think of yourself more highly than you ought to think, but think unto sobriety and just as God has distributed a share of the faith to each one. (Rom 12:3)

Self-indulgence
Woe to you, scribes and Pharisees, you hypocrites! For you clean what is outside the cup and the dish, but on the inside you are full of avarice and self-indulgence. (Matt 23:25)

Self-justification
He said to them: "You are the ones who justify yourselves in the sight of men. But God knows your hearts. For what is lifted up by men is an abomination in the sight of God. (Luk 16:15)

Self-praise
Let another praise you, and not your own mouth: an outsider, and not your own lips. (Pro 27:2)

Self-righteousness
He saved us, not by works of righteousness that we had done, but, in accord with his mercy, by the washing of regeneration and by the renovation of the Holy Spirit. (Tit 3:5)

For it is not through our righteousness that we offer requests before your face, but through the fullness of your compassion. (Dan 9:18)

Self-seeking
Therefore, all things whatsoever that you wish that men would do to you, do so also to them. For this is the law and the prophets. (Matt 7:12)

Sexual Sins
Do you not know that you are the Temple of God, and that the Spirit of God lives within you? But if anyone violates the Temple of God, God will destroy him. For the Temple of God is holy, and you are that Temple. (1 Cor 3:16-17)

Sloth
The way of the slothful is like a hedge of thorns. The way of the just is without offense. (Pro 15:19)

Smoking
If anyone violates the Temple of God, God will destroy him. For the Temple of God is holy, and you are that Temple. (1 Cor 3:17)

Stealing
Whoever was stealing, let him now not steal, but rather let him labor, working with his hands, doing what is good, so that he may have something to distribute to those who suffer need. (Eph 4:28)

Strife, Quarrel, Fights
Refrain from strife, and you will diminish your sins. For an ill-tempered man enflames conflict, and a sinful man troubles his friends, and he casts hostility into the midst of those who have peace. (Sir 28:8-9)

Superstition

Do not be led away by changing or strange doctrines. And it is best for the heart to be sustained by grace, not by foods. For the latter have not been as useful to those who walked by them. (Heb 13:9)

Swearing

Before all things, my brothers, do not choose to swear, neither by heaven, nor by the earth, nor in any other oath. But let your word 'Yes' be yes, and your word 'No' be no, so that you may not fall under judgment. (Jas 5:12)

Time (misuse of time)

See to it that you live carefully, not like the foolish, but like the wise: making the most of the time, because the days are evil. (Eph 5:15-16)

Unbelief

He was not able to perform any miracles there, except that he cured a few of the infirm by laying his hands on them. And he wondered, because of their unbelief, (Mrk 6:5-6)

Unforgiveness

A man holds on to anger against another man, and does he then expect healing from God? (Sir 28:3)

Worldliness

Do not choose to love the world, nor the things that are in the world. If anyone loves the world, the love of the Father is not in him. For all that is in the world-the desire of the flesh, and the desire of the eyes, and the pride of life-is not of the Father, but is of the world. (1 Jn 2:15-16)

Why do we Adore Jesus in the Blessed Sacrament?

It is an act of listening to Jesus
Each time, we spend time with Jesus at the Blessed Sacrament, we imitate Mary, who sat at the feet of Jesus and listened to him.

She had a sister, named Mary, who, while sitting beside the Lord's feet, was listening to his word. (Luk 10:39)

We find rest to our whole being
Jesus invites us to rest in his presence, which will give us the strength and energy to our whole being to face the challenges of life. Our soul, mind, and body will feel rested when we spend time with Jesus

Come to me, all you who labor and have been burdened, and I will give you rest. (Matt 11:28)

Jesus in the tabernacle fills our inner hunger and thirst
Jesus is the bread of life. The Eucharist is to the soul the way food is to the body. The food we eat sustains us with energy, vitamins, nutrients, and minerals. Similarly, Jesus, who is present in the blessed sacrament, fills the needs of our spiritual being.

I am the bread of life. Whoever comes to me shall not hunger, and whoever believes in me shall never thirst. (Jn 6:35)

It is an act of spending time with God
We show our love for someone by spending time with that person. Spending time with the one we love is one of the basic and primary requirements of love. We long to be with the one we love. Therefore, we express our love for Jesus by spending time with Him in the Blessed Sacrament.

When he returned to the camp, his minister Joshua, the son of Nun, a young man, did not withdraw from the Tabernacle. (Exo 33:11)

It is our personal time with the Lord
God wants to meet us in person and he waits for each one of us wanting to talk to us and share his gifts with us. Jesus waited by the well for the Samaritan woman and promised her the gift of the Holy Spirit. He waits for each one of us in the Blessed Sacrament to shower his heavenly gifts on us and to talk to us in person.

Jesus, being tired from the journey, was sitting in a certain way on the well. It was about the sixth hour. A woman of Samaria arrived to draw water. Jesus said to her, "Give me to drink." (Jn 4:6-7)

We find our intimacy in God's love
Jesus demonstrated the greatest love when he sacrificed himself on the cross for us while we were still sinners. Jesus invites us to a loving relationship and he pours his love into our hearts when we adore him in the Blessed Sacrament.

Through the abundance of your steadfast love, I will enter your house. I will show adoration toward your holy temple, in your fear. (Ps 5:7)

It is an act of gazing at Jesus
We are blessed to be looking at Jesus the way the people in the Gospel times were able to see his glory in human form.

My eyes are ever toward the Lord, for he will pull my feet from the snare. (Ps 25:15)

I have appeared in the sanctuary before you, in order to behold your virtue and your glory. (Ps 63:2)

We receive revelation about spiritual matters
Jesus fills us with his divine wisdom, knowledge, and understanding when we adore the Lord in the blessed sacrament. The two disciples on the way to Emmaus, were looking at life from the world's perspective. Jesus joined them and spent time with them and as a result, their spiritual eyes were opened and they were able to see their mission from God's perspective.

I considered, so that I might know this. It is a hardship before me, until I may enter into the Sanctuary of God, and understand it to its last part. (Ps 73:16-17)

Why do we Praise God?

Praise recognizes God as God
The Catechism of the Catholic Church gives three reasons why one must praise God. The foremost reason being that praise identifies us as God's creation and gives credit to God as the creator and the sustainer of the whole universe.

Praise is the form of prayer which recognizes most immediately that God is God. It lauds God for his own sake and gives him glory, quite beyond what he does, but simply because HE IS. It shares in the blessed happiness of the pure of heart who love God in faith before seeing him in glory. (CCC 2639)

Praise unites our spirit with the Holy Spirit
Each time we lift our hearts to praise God, we are uniting ourselves with the spirit of God who is given to us a gift and who reminds us that we are the children of God because of our faith in Jesus.

By praise, the Spirit is joined to our spirits to bear witness that we are children of God, testifying to the only Son in whom we are adopted and by whom we glorify the Father. (CCC 2639)

Praise lifts up all our prayers, needs, petitions to God
The Catechism also teaches that by praising God, we are lifting our everyday needs and petitions to God. Praise is a result oriented prayer. Praise draws the attention of God to our life situations.

Praise embraces the other forms of prayer and carries them toward him who is its source and goal: the "one God, the Father, from whom are all things and for whom we exist." (CCC 2639)

I will praise your name unceasingly, and I will praise it with thanksgiving, for my prayer was heeded. And you freed me from perdition, and you rescued me from the time of iniquity. (Sir 51:11)

Praise frees us from sinful inclinations
Praise has the power to help us overcome our sinful tendencies and desires. The book of Sirach, chapter 47, verse 10 and 11, gives us the assurance of God's intervention in our sinfulness, when we praise his holy name.

They would praise the holy name of the Lord, and magnify the sanctity of God, from early morning. The Lord took away his sins, and he exalted his power forever. And he gave him the covenant of the kingdom, and a throne of glory in Israel. (Sir 47:10-11)

Praise brings us into the presence of God

Praise makes God's presence alive in our lives. God longs to fill us with his presence and when long and thrist for him with our free will. Praise is a demonstration of our readiness to be filled and surrounded by God's presence.

Enter his gates with thanksgiving, his courts with praise, and acknowledge him. Bless his name. (Ps 100:4)

Praise frees us from negativity (Negative emotions)

God's presence comes with it advantages. God is full of love, joy, and peace. When we are filled with his presence, we too will experience the fulness of love, joy, and peace in us. We will freed of our negativity, heaviness, and the burdens of the heart. Praise fills us with his presence which in turn will drive our all our negative emotions.

I will praise the name of God with a song, and I will magnify him with praise. Let the oppressed see and rejoice. You who seek God, let your hearts revive (Ps 69:30,32)

Ps 30:4-5

Praise helps us overcome fears

Fear is an agent of Satan which he uses against people to keep them in chains and to prevent them from performing to their full potential. God does not want us to live in fear and he gives us a way to come our of our fears and timidity. Praise has the power to pull us our of our fears and insecurities.

In God, whose Word I praise. In God, I have put my trust. I will not fear what flesh can do to me. (Ps 56:4)

Praise heals our inner wounds

Praise does not make God bigger than who he is. Praise does not change God's stature but can do wonders for the one who praises him. When we exalt and glorify God's name, he in turn, intervenes in our lives and heals us body, mind, and soul.

Why are you sad, my soul? And why do you disquiet me? Hope in God, for I will again praise him: the salvation of my countenance. (Ps 41:5)

Praise is a demonstration of our faith (Praise releases our faith)

Are you in a faith crisis? Do you feel like you don't have enough faith to believe in God or seek God's help for your life's challenges and needs? The way to find faith when we most need it, is by praising God. Praise is a form of prayer that activates and releases our faith to believe in God and the great things that he can do for us. It is a proven and biblical method to grow and operate in faith.

They were walking in the midst of the flame, praising God and blessing the Lord. Then Azariah, while standing, prayed in this manner, and opening his mouth in the midst of the fire, he said: "Blessed are you, O Lord, the God of our fathers, and your name is praiseworthy and glorious for all ages. (Dan 3:24-26)

The Holy Spirit comes upon us when we praise God

Praise also activates the power of the Holy Spirit in us. God lavishes us with his Spirit when his name is praised and glorified.

While the musician was playing, the power of the Lord came on him. (2 Kgs 3:15)

Do not choose to be drunk with wine, for this is self-indulgence. Instead, be filled with the Holy Spirit, speaking among yourselves in psalms and hymns and spiritual canticles, singing and reciting psalms to the Lord in your hearts, giving thanks always for everything, in the name of our Lord Jesus Christ, to God the Father. (Eph 5:18-20)

Praise removes obstacles in our lives

Satan, because of his envy, causes obstructions for us and prevents us from receiving our God given blessings. Add to that, we also block our own blessings by our sinful lifestyle and disobedience to God's laws and commandments. Praise has the power to break those spiritual blocks and obstacles that hinder our blessings.

With all the people shouting, and the trumpets blaring, after the voice and the sound increased in the ears of the multitude, the walls promptly fell to ruin. (Josh 6:1-20)

We receive the anointing to speak God's Word when we praise God

Praise makes us the mouthpiece of God and transforms us into his ministers. We become the channels of God's grace and love to this unbelieving world.

While the musician was playing, the power of the Lord fell upon him, and he said: "Thus says the Lord: Make, in the channel of this torrent, pit after pit." (2 Kgs 3:15-16)

Praise delivers us from evil

Satan cannot stand or tolerate when God's name is praised or glorified, which forces him to flee. Therefore the best way to cast out the devil is by praising God.

Praising, I will call upon the Lord. And I will be saved from my enemies. (Ps 18:3)

Praise frees us from demonic oppression

Praise weakens the power of the evil one and his fallen angels over us. The demonic kingdom is defeated and forced to flee when God is praised.

I will praise the name of God with a song, and I will magnify him with praise. And it will please God more than a new calf producing horns and hoofs. Let the oppressed see and rejoice. (Ps 69:30-32)

We receive divine wisdom and knowledge when we praise God

God lavishes us with his wisdom and other spiritual gifts such as knowledge, understanding, and counsel, when we praise his holy name and give glory to who he is.

He set his eye upon their hearts, to reveal to them the greatness of his works, so that they might highly praise his holy name, and give glory to his wonders, so that they might declare the greatness of his works. In addition, he gave them knowledge and the law of life, as their inheritance. (Sir 17:7-9)

When God is praised, all those who plot evil against us will be defeated

The Bible is filled with stories where, when the people of Israel praised God, he gave them victory over their enemies and all those who attacked them. It is true to even this day. When we are threatened by people who consider us as their enemies, all we must do is praise God. He will not let the evil plots of people to succeed against us

When they had begun to sing praises, the Lord turned their ambushes upon themselves, that is, those of the sons of Ammon, and of Moab, and of mount Seir, who had gone forth so that they might fight against Judah. And they were struck down. (2 Chron 20:22-23)

God intervenes when we praise Him (miracles, wonders, healings, and blessings are released)

Whatever the situation may demand, either it be a miracle, or a healing, or a blessing, all one must do is praise God. God intervenes in the lives of his people and performs the needed work.

In the middle of the night, Paul and Silas were praying and praising God. And those who were also in custody were listening to them. Yet truly, there was a sudden earthquake, so great that the foundations of the prison were moved. And immediately all the doors were opened, and the bindings of everyone were released. (Acts 16:25-26)

Praise brings restoration

In the book of Baruch (Ch 2:32-34), we read about the Israelites who in their captivity, praised God and repented for their sins. God was moved by their contrition and restored everything that they had lost and he also liberated them from their captivity.

They will praise me in the land of their captivity, and will remember my name. And they will turn themselves away from their stiff back, and from their wicked deeds, for they will call to mind the way of their fathers, who sinned against me. And I will restore them to the land which I pledged to their fathers, Abraham, Isaac, and Jacob, and they will rule over it, and I will multiply them, and they will not be diminished. (Bar 2:32-34)

Praise brings comfort in times of suffering

We will receive comfort and consolation in times of pain and suffering when we praise God and glorify his name.

Give praise, O heavens! And exult, O earth! Let the mountains give praise with jubilation! For the Lord has consoled his people, and he will take pity on his suffering ones. (Is 49:13)

Praise strengthens us

We will be filled with supernatural strength and courage to face the challenges and tasks of this life when we praise God.

Then they all together praised the merciful Lord, and were strengthened in their souls, being prepared to break through not only men, but also the most ferocious beasts and walls of iron. (2 Mac 11:9)

More Titles from Gifted Books and Media

RETURN TO GOD
Confession Handbook

PREACHER'S HANDBOOK

SCRIPTURAL ROSARY
1000 Bible Verses

GOD'S PROMISES AND BLESSINGS FOR AN ABUNDANT LIFE

30 REASONS TO GO TO CONFESSION

EXAMINATION OF CONSCIENCE
For Teens

FREEDOM FROM PORN AND MASTURBATION

EXAMINATION OF CONSCIENCE
For Adults

SCRIPTURAL STATIONS OF THE CROSS

GODLY CHILD
Children's Guide to Catholic Living

EXAMINATION OF CONSCIENCE
For Children

TO JESUS WITH MARY
Scriptural Rosary on the Life and Ministry of Jesus

Now on Sale
Available in Paperback and Ebook
www.giftedbookstore.com

Made in the USA
Monee, IL
16 February 2023